TECHNICAL REPORT

T0164182

Identifying Arabic-Language Materials for Children That Promote Tolerance and Critical Thinking

Gail L. Zellman, Jeffrey Martini, Michal Perlman

Prepared for the Office of the Secretary of Defense

NATIONAL DEFENSE RESEARCH INSTITUTE

The research described in this report was prepared for the Office of the Secretary of Defense (OSD). The research was conducted within the RAND National Defense Research Institute, a federally funded research and development center sponsored by OSD, the Joint Staff, the Unified Combatant Commands, the Navy, the Marine Corps, the defense agencies, and the defense Intelligence Community under Contract W74V8H-06-C-0002.

Library of Congress Control Number: 2011923236

ISBN: 978-0-8330-5174-5

The RAND Corporation is a nonprofit institution that helps improve policy and decisionmaking through research and analysis. RAND's publications do not necessarily reflect the opinions of its research clients and sponsors.

RAND® is a registered trademark.

Published 2011 by the RAND Corporation
1776 Main Street, P.O. Box 2138, Santa Monica, CA 90407-2138
1200 South Hayes Street, Arlington, VA 22202-5050
4570 Fifth Avenue, Suite 600, Pittsburgh, PA 15213-2665
RAND URL: http://www.rand.org/
To order RAND documents or to obtain additional information, contact
Distribution Services: Telephone: (310) 451-7002;
Fax: (310) 451-6915; Email: order@rand.org

Preface

This document describes the creation of developmentally appropriate criteria used to identify and screen Arabic-language works for children that promote tolerance and critical thinking and also describes the characteristics of the materials that were found. It presents several examples of those works that met those criteria. It also discusses barriers that prevent the development and dissemination of more such works and suggests ways to address and overcome these barriers.

This research was sponsored by the Office of the Secretary of Defense (OSD), which had supported an earlier effort to identify adult materials that promote tolerance and critical thinking (Schwartz et al., 2009). It was conducted within the International Security and Defense Policy Center of the RAND National Defense Research Institute, a federally funded research and development center sponsored by the OSD, the Joint Staff, the Unified Combatant Commands, the Navy, the Marine Corps, the defense agencies, and the defense Intelligence Community.

For more information on the International Security and Defense Policy Center, see http://www.rand.org/nsrd/about/isdp.html or contact the director (contact information is provided on the web page).

Contents

Figures and Table

Summary

There is widespread awareness both inside and outside the Arab world that reform is necessary to further human development in the region.[1] One critical component of reform is the building of a knowledge society that supports and values the production, diffusion, and application of new knowledge and the expression of new ideas. A key aspect of a knowledge society is a well-educated citizenry open to new ideas, motivated and capable of challenging the ideas of others, and able to create important local knowledge.

One way to build these skills is to capitalize on the rich cultural resources already being produced in Arabic that reinforce tolerance by celebrating the region's cultural, religious, and ethnic diversity and that promote new ideas and support the development of critical thinking. The work described in this report is part of a broader effort to identify and disseminate materials whose messages encourage tolerance and support the development and use of critical thinking skills. This work, focused on identifying Arabic language materials targeted to children ages 4–14, arguably may be even more effective in promoting tolerance and critical thinking than earlier efforts directed toward adults (Schwartz et al., 2009). While a large social psychological literature attests to the fact that attitudes can be changed, this literature also finds that deep-seated, long-held attitudes that verge on or represent core values and morals are among the most difficult to alter. Moreover, by adulthood, it may be much more difficult to get people to consider new ideas that challenge long-held beliefs. As a result, most adults who acquire and engage with materials that promote tolerance and critical thinking already support their messages; getting these materials into the hands and minds of those who think differently poses enormous challenges.

In contrast, targeting youth has numerous advantages. First, works for children can offer constructive messages at a time when ideas about in-groups and out-groups are just forming; there is less need to counter intolerant beliefs. Second, tolerant messages can be (indeed, for the youngest children, must be) presented in a nonpolitical form that is less likely to upset parents or other authority figures. And third, the combination of the "youth bulge" in the Arab world and the fact that Arab children are far more likely than their parents to be literate translates into a much larger potential audience for children's materials than for adult materials.[2]

---

[1] The Arab Human Development Reports represent the most prominent calls for reform and greater attention to human development emanating from within the region. In addition, see el Baz (2007). For examples of specific initiatives, see Sakr (2008); Arab Republic of Egypt (2007); and The Jordan Education Initiative (2007).

[2] The spread between adult and youth literacy in the Arab world is quite large. Particularly large differences in literacy rates among adults (everyone over the age of 15) versus youth (just those aged 15–24) are found in the following countries: Algeria (69.9 percent versus 90.1 percent); Egypt (71.4 percent versus 84.9 percent); Morocco (52.3 percent versus 70.5 percent); Sudan (60.9 percent versus 77.2 percent); Tunisia (74.3 percent versus 94.3 percent). All data are from the 2009 Arab Human Development Report.

Using developmental psychology theory and research, we determined what messages, in what form, are most understandable to children of different ages and what presentational elements make materials engaging and therefore potentially persuasive to children. We used what we learned to develop a set of criteria for identifying and screening children's works that foster tolerance and critical thinking.

Of the 104 works that were identified and screened, 68 met those criteria and form our final repository. The bulk of the collection is made up of written works and is dominated by short stories. The print focus reflects the limited availability of locally developed works available in other types of media. Specifically, there are very few indigenously produced cartoons in the Arab world—and fewer still promote the values on which our efforts focused. More than half (52 percent) of the materials collected were authored or produced in the four countries of the Levant—Jordan, Lebanon, Palestine, and Syria—despite strong efforts to ensure geographic diversity across the Arab world.

The rejected works generally paid insufficient attention to constructive themes; particularly in materials for the youngest group (ages 4–6), the value of obedience often overshadowed messages about tolerance or support for critical thinking. Materials were disqualified that promoted intergroup understanding at the expense of another group. For example, one rejected book encouraged unity between Christian and Muslim Palestinians in order to unite against Israeli occupation.[3] Another rejection criterion concerned the outcome of the critical thinking process portrayed. If the end result was greater adherence to a traditional belief system or support for intolerance, then the material was not accepted.

The collected works validate the view of Arab scholars that important creative materials are being produced in the region despite, or perhaps because of, the political and intellectual challenges that artists confront. Indeed, we found a significant body of children's literature indigenous to the Arab region that promotes tolerance and critical thinking. A number of works even took on taboo or otherwise sensitive subjects—e.g., a young child whose divorced parents share custody and cooperate in parenting him; a teenage boy who is abused by his alcoholic father.

The collection points as well to a number of weaknesses in the supply of constructive works. The most obvious is the often poor production quality of books published in the region. Poor-quality paper, printing, and illustrations (some books had missing pages) and the absence of illustrations in some materials for the youngest age group make many of these materials unattractive and unengaging. Online content was beset with its own problems: There were numerous broken links, examples of authors posting text but not illustrations, or text abruptly cutting off before the end of the story. Poor print production quality is probably best explained by the perceived need to keep books affordable, particularly in poorer countries like Egypt. Poor presentation of online content probably reflects the fact that authors are forced to post their own content rather than having dedicated IT support from a publisher.

A number of barriers exist to increasing both the supply and quality of these materials. High illiteracy and poverty rates reduce the demand for such works (UNDP, 2003). Earlier RAND work that focused on adult materials noted there are few bookstores and few public libraries in the region, and more "liberal" books are banned while intolerant literature is subsidized. Little taste for leisure reading further discourages demand for such materials (Schwartz

---

3   Najlā' Nasīr Bashūr, *Sha'nūnat al-'Īd* ("Palm Sunday"), Beirut: Mu'sasat Tāla: 2004.

et al., 2009). Although our research did not allow us to systematically examine barriers to the production and dissemination of materials that support tolerance, the collection process revealed a number of barriers, including limited access to many of these materials, poor production values, and unclear copyrights. Previous RAND work on education reform in the Gulf region suggested additional barriers to the dissemination of these materials to children. Specifically, rigid, centrally controlled education curricula whose content might not change for decades may not accommodate works for children with messages of tolerance. Despite parents' importance in conveying attitudes, values, and support for literacy, we know little about their role in promoting media use, reading to their young children, and conveying messages about tolerance and support for critical thinking. RAND's education reform work in the Gulf suggests that parents tend to view the schools and educators as the experts in imparting key cultural values; they neither seek nor readily accept this role for themselves (Zellman et al., 2009).

To encourage the development and dissemination of materials that support constructive messages, it is critical to systematically examine gaps in our knowledge. In particular, we lack good market data about children's publishing and particularly about the role of copyright issues, although failure to develop and enforce copyright laws is generally recognized by those in the region as a serious problem (UNDP, 2003). We also lack a clear understanding of piracy issues, which were informally reported to us in the course of our work as a compelling contributor to the widespread reluctance to produce high-cost, high-quality television productions.

It is important as well to look at key cultural institutions to determine how they can help to get materials with constructive themes into the hands of children. A first effort might focus on examining the openness of schools and education ministries to including such materials in their curricula or libraries. A number of countries in the region have begun to reform their education systems (UNDP, 2003). In a more open education space, these materials might find a place if they were better known, if teachers could receive training on how to integrate them into lessons and other activities, and if they were more accessible.

There could be considerable payoff from an exploration of the role that parents play in encouraging literacy and tolerance in their children. Research consistently identifies parents as the primary sources of influence on a host of outcomes; parents serve as the gatekeepers for information and conveyors of values. Little is known about perceived parental roles or models of socialization in the Arab world, although such knowledge is critical in understanding how parents might help to promote open-mindedness, tolerance, and critical thinking in their children.

In the short run, it is important to make the materials we identified widely available. One approach would be to make our catalog available on the Web. It might be possible as well to work with libraries, bookstores, and cultural centers in the region to bring these materials to a wider audience. It might also be worthwhile to think about ways to make these materials accessible to Arabic-speaking children in the United States. One approach might be to place these materials in public library and school library collections in areas with a high concentration of Arabic speakers (e.g., the greater Detroit and Washington, D.C., areas). Finally, it would be most worthwhile, given the low levels of literacy and small amount of leisure reading in much of the Arab world, to find ways to convert or adapt printed works with constructive themes for other media, particularly television, given the high penetration of satellite television programming in the region. Airing such programming during Ramadan would be particularly attractive given the cultural norm of families watching television series after breaking the fast.

Dissemination of works with constructive themes requires consideration of current barriers and supports. Efforts to adapt printed works to other media may require that attention be paid to mitigating the disincentives for doing so, most particularly widespread copyright violations and pirating of such materials. Regional authors, publishers, educators, and policymakers are best positioned to disseminate these works to potential users and to develop ways to capture and promote more such materials, since successful and sustainable reform must come from within (UNDP, 2003). A solid dissemination strategy should build on local institutions such as ministries of education and nongovernment organizations. Attention also should be paid to the role that parents currently play and might play in the future in supporting such works. Our collection, which clearly demonstrates the richness of regional materials, hopefully will encourage these efforts.

Acknowledgments

The authors wish to thank all those who made this study possible. First, we would like to thank Jennifer Bryson, from OSD-Policy, who initially proposed and oversaw the project. Thanks go as well to Nermine Nakhla, who took Jennifer's place when she left the government, and to Benjamin Riley III, who supported the project throughout.

This research also benefited enormously from our colleagues' previous study of Arabic language adult materials that support tolerance and critical thinking. And although our follow-on effort sought to improve on the study approach used in the initial effort, we drew much wisdom and support from their earlier work in this area.

We also want to thank Maryam Kia-Keating, Badia Madbak, and Fadia Hoteit, who carefully reviewed our coding criteria and helped us think through their relevance for materials written and produced in the region and for the region's children. Our work benefited enormously from our discussions with authors, publishers, and distributors of creative works in the Middle East, as well as from producers in the United States. We are most grateful to all of them for contributing their views and comments. We also wish to thank our RAND colleagues, Rebecca Bouchebel, Walid Kildani, and Nadia Oweidat, for their excellent sleuthing and thoughtful coding of the works. Special thanks go to Christopher Dirks for his valuable assistance with many aspects of the project, particularly the development of the database, and to Dalia Dassa Kaye for her many insightful ideas about how best to pursue this work. Thanks go as well to Roald Euller for his help in assessing inter-rater reliability. We are grateful to Julie Taylor of RAND and Regan Gurung of the University of Wisconsin Green Bay for their careful reviews of this report. Finally, we owe thanks to Michael Lostumbo and James Dobbins of the RAND International Security and Defense Policy Center for their generous support of this work.

Abbreviations

MENA   Middle East and North Africa

OSD   Office of the Secretary of Defense

SLT   social learning theory

tweens   children between the ages of 10 and 13

CHAPTER ONE

Background

There is general consensus both inside and outside the Arab world that reform is necessary in the region to promote human development there. One critical component of reform is the advancement of knowledge and the development of a knowledge society that supports and values the production and dissemination of new knowledge and the expression of new ideas (UNDP, 2003). A key aspect of a knowledge society is a well-educated citizenry that is open to new ideas and is capable of and motivated to create new local knowledge through the use of its critical thinking capacity.

One approach to developing such a citizenry is to capitalize on the cultural resources already being produced in Arabic, which are part of a rich cultural and intellectual heritage. These materials, available in a variety of media, can help to promote new ideas and support the development of critical thinking. The work described in this report is part of a broader effort to identify and disseminate materials whose messages encourage tolerance and open-mindedness and support the development and use of critical thinking skills.

The work described in this report focused on the collection and screening of materials for children ages 4–14. This child-focused effort follows on the work done by RAND colleagues to identify adult materials that further these goals in the Middle East and North Africa (MENA) region. That earlier work (Schwartz et al., 2009) found a substantial number of little-known materials that focused on the promotion of tolerance and critical thinking; indeed, study staff found many authors who were deliberately producing novels, plays, short stories, and movies designed to address the very goals that fueled the RAND work. At the same time, our RAND colleagues identified a number of significant barriers to the production and distribution of these works, an issue we return to at several points in this report. Among the key ones: Such materials are often banned, while those that promote intolerance are widely available and may be subsidized; copyright protections are often poorly enforced or nonexistent; outlets for these works are limited.

The focus on materials targeted to children ages 4–14 arguably may be even more valuable in promoting open-mindedness and critical thinking than efforts directed toward adults. While a large social psychological literature attests to the fact that attitudes can be changed, this literature also finds that deep-seated, long-held attitudes that verge on or represent core values and morals are among the most difficult to alter. Moreover, by adulthood, people's attitudes already are formed; it may be much more difficult to get people to be open to new ideas that challenge long-held beliefs or new ways of thinking and problem-solving. As a result, most of those who acquire and engage with materials that promote tolerance and critical thinking already support their messages; getting these materials into the hands and minds of those who think differently is very difficult.

In contrast, targeting younger demographics has numerous advantages. First, works for children can offer constructive messages at a time when ideas about in-groups and out-groups are just forming; there is less need to counter intolerant beliefs. Second, tolerant messages can be (indeed for the youngest children must be) presented in a nonpolitical form that is less likely to upset parents or other authority figures. And third, the combination of the "youth bulge" in the Arab world and the fact that Arab children are far more likely than their parents to be literate, translates into a much larger potential audience for children's materials than for adult materials.

Identifying and disseminating these works is of particular importance in the Arab world because, with notable exceptions, the educational environment in the Middle East does not foster critical thinking or tolerance.[1] Indeed, traditional education systems in this part of the world generally rely on rote memorization and, in both process and content, preach deference to authority (UNDP, 2003; Gregg, 2005; Brewer et al., 2007).

Objectives

Our work involved four key tasks. First, we sought to determine what messages, in what form, are most understandable to children of different ages, and what makes materials engaging and therefore potentially persuasive for children. To do this, we reviewed relevant developmental theories and empirical research on the socialization of tolerance and critical thinking. This work helped us to identify key content and presentational factors that make materials compelling to children and their messages as acceptable as possible.

Second, we used the theory and research-based findings we examined in pursuing our first task to develop a set of criteria that would direct our collection and review of promising works. By clarifying how the criteria applied at different ages, Arabic-speaking staff could begin to search for materials that might meet these criteria.

Third, we cast a wide net in hopes of identifying lesser-known and difficult-to-find materials that met our research-based criteria. We screened each material to determine whether it met our inclusion criteria. Those materials that met criteria were included in our database.

Finally, we developed an illustrated catalogue that could be easily shared with the aim of making these works better-known and more accessible; keeping in mind that while U.S. institutions can help identify promising materials and the creators of them, dissemination is likely to be far more effective if it comes in the form of local initiatives.

Organization of the Report

In Chapter Two, we present a review of the literature on the development and expression of tolerance and critical thinking in children ages 4–14. The literature review focuses on early learning about in-groups, out-groups, and tolerance; we also examine the literature on the socialization and expression of tolerance later in childhood and on the contextual factors that promote and inhibit the expression of tolerance. We then touch briefly on efforts to teach tol-

---

[1] Qatar is a significant exception because of its K–12 education reform, one of whose key goals is to inculcate critical thinking skills (Brewer et al., 2007, and Zellman et al., 2009).

erance. Finally, we examine key developmental theories and draw from them lessons about content that are likely to promote tolerance. In Chapter Three, we discuss the development of the screening criteria that we applied in searching for appropriate materials. We focus the discussion on developmental stages and corresponding abilities drawn from developmental theory. In Chapter Four, we discuss the materials search process and describe the collection we amassed, offering an example of a work that met criteria for each study age group. We analyze the collection's strengths and weaknesses and discuss the reasons for rejection of some collected works. In Chapter Five, we discuss our conclusions and suggest future directions. Appendix A examines the effectiveness of a range of interventions that attempt to socialize tolerance and critical thinking. Appendix B contains our screening criteria. Appendix C presents the coding form and the manual we developed to help coders produce consistent ratings.

CHAPTER TWO

The Development and Expression of Tolerance and Critical Thinking in Children Ages 4–14

Introduction

Tolerance and critical thinking are attitudinal and behavioral dispositions that are believed to be important predictors of the extent to which individuals support inclusive public policies, regimes that vilify outsiders, political leaders who espouse violence and separatism, and societies that encourage cooperation and human rights (e.g., Sullivan and Transue, 1999; Vogt, 1997). While support for tolerant and intolerant public policies is fueled by contemporary media and peer interactions (Berry, 1993; Cortes, 1995), it is generally agreed that tolerance and critical thinking skills are embedded far earlier, well before children understand the contemporary political or social scene. Indeed, these early attitudes and predispositions are believed to have their roots in the preschool period, and are fostered or altered as children mature and can better absorb the lessons provided by their families, their religious leaders, and their teachers.

This chapter explores the literature on the development of tolerance and critical thinking and their opposites: intolerance and lack of critical thinking. It also presents several key developmental theories and how they relate to the development of these attributes. The socialization of these predispositions is important because they form a mindset or filter through which the events of the day are viewed and frequently form the basis of decisions that individuals make about how to treat their neighbors, raise their children, and respond to political and religious issues, such as the permissibility of coeducation and mixed-faith marriages. In the case of critical thinking, these skills provide ways for individual citizens to understand the events of the day and to draw their own conclusions about them. Skilled critical thinkers are less likely to accept political rhetoric on its face, and are more likely to examine the evidence and come to their own conclusions about the rightness of assertions about the behavior and rights of out-groups. Tolerant attitudes support critical thinking by enabling individuals to keep their minds open and free of judgment as they examine information prior to drawing conclusions; critical thinking supports tolerance by enabling people to consider a range of ideas and draw their own, reasoned conclusions (Marshalidis, 2001).

Although this literature review draws almost exclusively from Western psychological literature and key psychological theories developed by Western psychologists, we took a number of steps to ensure that the cultural specificities of the Arab world were considered. First, for the sake of completeness, we examined cultural analyses of the Arab world (e.g., Gregg, 2005). Second and more important, staff members with deep familiarity with the Arab world were consulted as this review went forward; the coding categories that resulted (described in Chapter Three) were strongly influenced by their input. Finally, we relied on several education experts from the region to review the screening criteria and to speak more generally about the cognitive and moral development of children in the Arab world. Our challenge was to take into account what is unique about the culture and context of the Arab world while avoiding the trap of "essentializing" Arabs, particularly given that cognitive development is generally agreed to be a generic process that transcends religion, ethnicity, and culture. Influential theorists, such as Chomsky (1976), have argued that language acquisition is innate and follows universal trajectories; this view has received some empirical support (e.g., Pinker, 1994). Nevertheless, it is important to note that the heavily Western origin of the literature and theories represents a significant limitation on how much the results can be generalized to non-Western cultures.

We undertook this work to contribute to a better understanding of the development of tolerance and critical thinking over the course of children's development. More immediately, this work guided the development of a set of screening criteria that we intended to use in the identification and examination of original Arabic language materials. These criteria would help us determine the extent to which the collected materials foster these attributes in children (see Chapter Three for a discussion of the translation of theories into criteria and for a description of the criteria we developed). The review that follows helped us understand how these dispositions are socialized and the abilities that children have at different ages to absorb key messages. This understanding, in turn, enabled us to develop a set of criteria to use in selecting materials and determining their age-appropriateness and message. By basing our criteria on developmental theory and empirical research, we believe that the materials selected are more likely to have their intended effect: to promote the development of tolerance and critical thinking. Understanding the trajectory of cognitive, moral, and emotional development from the early years (ages 4–6) through childhood (ages 7–10) and into adolescence (ages 11–14) could facilitate the selection of materials that children would understand in the ways that their authors intended. This also enabled us to pinpoint story lines, design features, and media attributes that are more likely to be understood and accepted by children at different ages. Ideally, we would have liked to test our criteria by exposing children to these works and examining their reactions. However, this effort was beyond the scope of our work.

In the course of our examination of child development over this period, we uncovered a large literature on interventions designed to promote tolerance and critical thinking in school settings. While this research is not immediately relevant, we include it in Appendix A for interested readers.

This chapter is made up of three sections. We begin with an overview of the literature and theory concerning the development of tolerance, intolerance, and critical thinking. We then present key developmental theories that provide important guidance concerning how best to support the development of tolerance and critical thinking in children. Having introduced those theories, in the third section we identify key developmental stages and align them with the theories. This enabled us to articulate the cognitive, emotional, and social skills and abilities relevant to the development of critical thinking and tolerance that children develop over time. (A table of abilities by age is presented in Appendix B to help clarify how tolerance-relevant development is viewed in the context of these theories.) This material is background for Chapter Three, in which we present and briefly discuss the resulting screening criteria and the process we undertook to refine the criteria and ensure coding consistency among multiple raters.

The Development of Critical Thinking, Tolerance, and Intolerance

Before delving into the literature, it is important to define the key terms and concepts on which this work focuses.

Critical Thinking

Critical thinking is the intellectually disciplined process of actively conceptualizing, applying, analyzing, synthesizing, and/or evaluating information gathered from, or generated by, observation, experience, reflection, reasoning, or communication, as a guide to belief and action. It is defined as the "deliberate use of skills and strategies that increase the probability of a desirable outcome" (Halpern, 1998, p. 449). Critical thinking is based on universal intellectual values that transcend subject matter divisions: clarity, accuracy, precision, consistency, relevance, sound evidence, good reasons, depth, breadth, and fairness. It entails the examination of those structures or elements of thought implicit in all reasoning: purpose, problem, or question; assumptions, concepts, empirical grounding; reasoning leading to conclusions, implications and consequences; objections from alternative viewpoints; and frame of reference. As noted above, critical thinking can apply to almost any subject matter and thus is part of scientific thinking, mathematical thinking, and historical thinking.

Critical thinking is generally viewed as the ability to decide, independent of reward and punishment, between right and wrong in the moral realm and between truth and falsehood in the intellectual realm (Piaget, 1948; 1983). Such abilities should be a central goal of education (Kamii, 1991).

Critical thinking can be seen as having two components (Scriven and Paul, n.d.):

1. A set of skills that support the generation and processing of information and beliefs.
2. The habit of using that skill set to guide behavior, based on an intellectual commitment to finding the best solutions to problems and basing beliefs in information.

Critical thinking based on these components and habits is contrasted with

- the mere acquisition and retention of information
- the mere possession of a set of skills
- the mere use of those skills (as an "exercise") without integrating their results into actions, beliefs, or solutions.

Like many other skills, critical thinking has both a skill component and a motivation component, although the skill component is far more often discussed in the literature. Yet Giancarlo, Blohm, and Urdan (2004) note that some students who are able to think critically often choose not to utilize this skill.[1] One reason is that employing critical thinking takes effort. Further, critical thinking may not be reinforced if conclusions run counter to shared beliefs. Solof and Houtz (1991) report age-related increases in critical thinking ability among students in grades K–4, with age differences becoming significant in grade 3.

---

[1] Concerns about students' unwillingness to engage this skill led Giancarlo et al. to develop a new instrument, the California Measure of Mental Motivation.

Tolerance

Tolerance has been defined as a fair, objective, and permissive attitude toward those whose opinions, practices, race, religion, nationality, etc., differ from one's own; freedom from bigotry. It also extends to the acceptance of opinions and practices, divorced to some degree from individuals, and may be defined as a fair, objective, and permissive attitude toward opinions and practices that differ from one's own. These definitions imply a more passive assessor: People or opinions are presented, and the tolerant person treats them with objectivity and respect. Tolerance may sometimes have a more active dimension, defined as having an interest in and concern for ideas, opinions, practices, etc., foreign to one's own; a liberal, nondogmatic viewpoint.[2]

Interestingly, a final definition of tolerance speaks to endurance: the power or capacity of an organism to tolerate unfavorable environmental conditions.[3] Tolerance in this definition is not the absence of prejudice but rather a separate construct that emphasizes forbearance, or "putting up with" (Verkuyten and Slooter, 2008). In this sense, this fourth definition is quite relevant to the social science understanding of the concept.

Verkuyten and Slooter argue that tolerance is crucial because it is the first and necessary step toward civility. Indeed, tolerance is considered foundational for democracy and a just society (Sullivan and Transue, 1999). Verkuyten and Slooter quote Vogt (1997, p. xviii), who argues:

> Tolerance is vitally important because of the inevitability of diversity and the apparent inevitability of stereotyping, bias and prejudice. But discrimination and persecution are not inevitable. Tolerance keeps negative attitudes and beliefs from becoming negative actions.

Literature on Tolerance

Tolerance is generally agreed to include attitudinal predispositions, specific attitudes, and a behavioral component that leads to the expression of tolerant or intolerant attitudes in defined situations. While the literature is consistent in viewing tolerance as a set of attitudes and beliefs that are learned (e.g., Simard and Wong, 2004) through family socialization, peer interaction, and personal experiences, these three aspects of tolerance are assumed to rely on somewhat different dynamics for their development and expression. For example, socialization of predispositions toward tolerance and intolerance are assumed to develop early; the focus of studies that examine these predispositions is generally the family. Understanding the expression of tolerance leads to more attention to the context, including characteristics of the actors being judged and the operation of social norms.

Early Learning About Tolerance

Early childhood is a critical period for the development of children's beliefs about critical aspects of the world around them, like the belief in God and divine creation of the universe (Bloom, 2007). Thus, it may provide a critical window for the instilling of attitudes about other groups. The general view in the literature is that attitudes about differences and about

---

[2]   See http://dictionary.reference.com/browse/tolerance, accessed December 22, 2009.

[3]   See http://wordnetweb.princeton.edu/perl/webwn, accessed December 22, 2009.

tolerance begin to be formed during the preschool period and are fairly well solidified by adolescence (Perkins and Ritchhart, 2004). Grouping along in-group-out-group boundaries starts young. Affective and attitudinal dispositions toward minorities have been documented in past research with preschoolers, demonstrating that the basis for the social institution of prejudice is in place early in social development (Popp, Fu, and Warrell, 1981; Spencer and Markstrom-Adams, 1990). Research indicates that by age 5, many white American children attribute negative characteristics to black Americans and positive characteristics to white Americans (Bigler and Liben, 1993; Doyle and Aboud, 1995). Popp, Fu, and Warrell (1981) find similar developmental processes concerning reactions to physical disability. They report that when rating slides and videotapes of children, preschool children prefer able-bodied children to disabled ones.

Classic doll studies conducted by Mamie and Kenneth Clark (1947) revealed that children respond to racial differences as early as 3 years of age, with both white and black children preferring white dolls. Since then, a growing body of research confirms the awareness and responsiveness of young children to cues of diversity (Clark, Hocevar, and Dembo, 1980; Garcia-Coll and Vazquez Garcia, 1995; Goodman, 1952; Spencer and Markstrom-Adams, 1990). By 3 or 4 years of age, many children are able to categorize people based on salient cues such as gender, race, or in certain cases, ability (Garcia-Coll and Vazquez Garcia, 1995; Katz, 1983; Ramsey and Myers, 1990), and children often choose friends based on these categorizations (Ramsey and Myers, 1990; Ramsey, 1991). Attitudes toward categories like color start to form and develop during the preschool years (Crooks, 1970; Goodman, 1964; Katz, 1983). However, Aboud (2003) notes that standardized measures of prejudice that reveal high levels of prejudice and ethnocentric bias in the preschool years may mask important subtleties. In-group bias in young children may reflect in-group favoritism, out-group prejudice, or both. She gave children between ages 4 and 7 an attitude assessment that partially decouples in-group favoritism and out-group prejudice, and found that the two feelings were highly correlated among children attending a race-homogeneous school. However, this was not the case among children attending a race-heterogeneous school. Strong in-group favoritism developed by age five; prejudice against out-groups was weaker. But the strong in-group preference may cause out-group members to suffer by comparison. Aboud's findings are consistent with Allport's (1954) contact hypothesis, which stipulates that under certain conditions prejudice is diminished when members of majority and minority group members have ongoing contact with one another. Interestingly, even imagined positive contact (i.e., mental simulation) can reduce prejudice toward members of an out-group (Crisp and Turner, 2009). Findings about the positive effects of imagined contact suggest that it may be possible to reduce prejudice by exposing children to positive views of out-group members through books and other forms of media.

The fact that these attitudes and predispositions develop so early has suggested to some psychologists that the transmission mechanism may precede modeling and imitation, described below, and inhere in the sorts of childrearing approaches practiced by parents. In particular, developmental theorists suggest that authoritarian childrearing practices may predispose children toward obedience and discourage critical thinking (e.g., Baumrind, 1967, 1971). Authoritarian childrearing practice refers to a childrearing approach that is high in coercive control, low in information, and quite restrictive in terms of children's autonomy and that discourages critical thinking (Adorno et al., 1950). Authoritarian parenting is an approach that emphasizes acceptance of authority and discourages questioning of rules or prescribed values. The classic example of a parenting strategy an authoritarian parent might use is telling a child to do something; when the child asks why he or she has to perform the specified task, the authoritarian parent says, "because I said so." Authoritarian child-rearing practices have been identified as an important aspect of childrearing in the Arab world. The 2003 Arab Human Development Report asserts "the most common style of child rearing within the Arab family is the authoritarian accompanied by the overprotective" (p. 51). Together, the report asserts, these practices reduce children's independence and initiative, suppress a child's inquisitiveness, and discourage independent critical thinking.

Baumrind and others focus on the ideal of authoritative parents, who are high in control but also high in warmth. Authoritative parents, faced with the same question from their child about why he or she had to do a particular task, might explain the reasons for the request and answer the child's questions while still ensuring that the task is done. Research finds that children exposed to authoritative parents demonstrate high self-esteem and little antisocial behavior in American preschools. The 2003 UNDP report asserts the same connection in the MENA region, citing research showing that children who have been brought up by firm parents (as contrasted with authoritarian or permissive parents) demonstrate greater psychological and social adaptation and perform better in school (Buri, 1988).

Learning About Tolerance Later On

As children develop, there are more opportunities for direct imitation of attitudes, beliefs, and behaviors. A large literature examines the degree to which the attitudes of parents and children toward out-groups are correlated. These correlations, of course, include both the effects of parenting style and imitation. White and Gleitzman (2006) found that the prejudice scores of the 93 adolescents in their study were significantly correlated with those of their parents. Higher levels of cohesion, adaptability, and communication in these families were significantly related to low levels of prejudice in adolescents and fathers. O'Bryan, Fishbein and Ritchey (2004) found that the influence of mothers and fathers on the intolerance of their young adolescent children varied by issue area, with, for example, mothers exerting more influence on attitudes toward race and obesity, while fathers exerted more influence over views of homosexuality. But like White and Gleitzman (2006) and many others, they found that when prejudice was measured more generally, Western parents exerted an important and equal influence on the tendency toward intolerance.

Out-group distinctions present in preschool generally continue throughout childhood and adolescence. But there is some evidence of change as well. Enright and Lapsley (1981) have described a developmental progression from generally intolerant attitudes during the childhood years toward increasingly tolerant judgments during adolescence (see also Enright et al., 1984). Other studies have also found age-related increases in tolerance (e.g., Thalhammer et al., 1994).

At least some of the increased tolerance that has been found as children age may be explained by the fact that they are becoming more educated over time. Verkuyten and Slooter (2008), like many other researchers, found an association between level of education and tolerance, with better-educated students expressing more tolerance, even given the truncated range of education represented in their study. Had a broader range of education been represented, the authors note, differences would probably have been greater. Verkuyten and Slooter speculate that education is associated with higher levels of tolerance because education increases cognitive sophistication, which is marked by better reasoning skills, cognitive flexibility, and greater knowledge. Hastie (2007) notes that higher education leads to liberalization in students' social and political attitudes and discusses two hypotheses that have been proposed to explain these effects: self-selection and socialization. In the first case, people choose academic disciplines whose views most closely match their own; in the second, people change their views to align with those of their discipline. Substantial differences in level of liberalism across academic discipline support these hypotheses. Change occurs when people's attitudes begin to align with those of the people around them and when they acquire specific, discipline-relevant knowledge. However, there are also studies that do not find increases in tolerance as children age. For example, Wainryb (1991, 1993) and Verkuyten and Slooter (2008) found that older adolescents are actually less tolerant than younger ones. One reason for inconsistent findings concerning the relationship between age and tolerance, according to Verkuyten and Slooter (2008), is that in these developmental stage studies, tolerance is typically conceptualized and treated as a single, global construct. Often, the measures used in these studies ask subjects to judge the personal worth of dissenting individuals; other dimensions of tolerance are not considered. Studies that do take different aspects of tolerance into account, e.g., context, type of activity described, nature of group membership, give a more complex picture of age differences with tolerance and intolerance coexisting at all ages (e.g., Wainryb, Shaw, and Maianu, 1998; Wainryb et al., 2001).

Tolerance levels may also change over time in response to changes in the political or social context. Dawes and Finchilescu (2002), using cross-sectional data from pre-apartheid and post-apartheid studies of black prejudice, found that among white South African high school students ages 14 and 17, already high levels of prejudice displayed in an earlier study conducted before the end of apartheid increased with the emergence of majority rule in the new post-apartheid state. Views of the new state, not surprisingly, were associated with the level of racism reported. Blacks in these studies displayed out-group preference toward whites, with increased levels of rejection of other black groups in the post-apartheid data.

Work by Crandall, Eshleman, and O'Brien (2002) underscores the importance of social norms, a key contextual variable, in expressing prejudice. In a series of studies in which they manipulated social norms, they found that the expression of prejudice toward a large number of different groups, including evaluating scenarios of discrimination and reacting to hostile jokes, was highly correlated with social approval of that expression. They suggest that suppression of prejudice may occur when group norms do not support prejudice. Haidt (2001) argues that this phenomenon often applies to moral judgments as well. Although moral judgments are believed to be the product of moral reasoning, Haidt argues that they are more influenced by social and cultural influences; moral reasoning is a post hoc construction applied *after* a culture-based judgment is made.

Contextual Factors in the Expression of Tolerance

A number of researchers have examined the effects of context, broadly defined, on the expression of tolerance and prejudice. In general, these studies point to the many subtleties involved in the expression of tolerance. For example, in their sample of Dutch adolescents, Verkuyten and Slooter (2008) found that the participants generally expressed moderate levels of tolerance. However, when subjects made multiple judgments about a range of attitudes and actions, the different judgments were not strongly associated; a single dimension of tolerance did not emerge. They also found that, in making judgments about the level of tolerance, adolescents take into account various aspects of what they are asked to tolerate—for example, behavior or beliefs, the degree to which the behavior (e.g., wearing of the head scarf) conflicts with adolescents' own values, the extremity of the behavior (e.g., burning the national flag versus petition-ing for rights), and the characteristics of the individuals engaged in the behavior. The charac-teristics of actors also affect judgments. For example, Verkuyten and Slooter (2008) found that in all their scenarios, their Dutch subjects expressed more tolerance toward Dutch actors than toward Muslim ones, even when they were portrayed as engaging in the same behavior.

Wainryb et al. (2001) found similar variety in their more age-diverse subjects. Thinking did not become more uniformly tolerant over the age range they studied (3rd and 7th graders and college students). Instead, subjects' views varied by type of belief and the characteristics of the people portrayed. At all ages, subjects found some disagreements acceptable and others not. Similarly, Wainryb, Shaw, and Maianu (1998) found consistent patterns across all age groups in their study in levels of tolerance, depending on the nature of the action being judged: more tolerance for dissenting beliefs than their expression; more tolerance for expression than belief-directed actions; and more tolerance for actors than acts.

Wright, Cullum, and Schwab (2008) analyzed the dimensions of moral conviction that may help to explain why age differences in tolerance may not emerge. They note that much dissension arises from disagreements about whether certain issues—e.g., environmental pres-ervation, abortion—are matters of personal choice or of morality. This distinction matters: Researchers in a variety of fields have reported that people are more intolerant of divergent attitudes when they involve moral issues rather than nonmoral ones. Wright, Cullum, and Schwab (2008) suggest that the reasons for this intolerance may be based in emotion or cog-nition. Skitka, Bauman, and Sargis (2005), for example, found that the strength of moral convictions predicted level of tolerance for and preferred social and physical distance from people who did not share subjects' moral conviction. Wright, Cullum, and Schwab (2008) argue that one reason for the association between strong moral beliefs and intolerance is that moral beliefs are largely affective and have a strong emotional charge. Indeed, research finds that strong attitudes are more resistant to change and that the holders of strong attitudes are more intolerant of those who hold dissimilar attitudes (Cantril, 1946; Downing, Judd, and Brauer, 1992). From a more cognitive perspective, moral beliefs may be viewed by their hold-ers as objective and self-evident (Skitka, Bauman, and Sargis, 2005). Consequently, those who do not subscribe to those self-evident beliefs are viewed quite negatively. Wright, Cullum, and Schwab (2008) found that both of these dimensions contribute to intolerance. Their college student subjects were more tolerant of divergent nonmoral attitudes (self-classified) than of divergent moral attitudes. Those with stronger moral beliefs were more intolerant. They also found that subjects acted on these beliefs. For example, subjects shared fewer raffle tickets with others who were believed to have divergent moral attitudes than with others whose nonmoral beliefs differed from theirs.

These studies suggest that the content and nature of the actions and actors in question, the apparent social implications of expressing tolerance or prejudice, and the dimension of tolerance measured all make a difference in the degree to which subjects express tolerance or behave in a tolerant way.

Teaching Tolerance and Critical Thinking

Much of the empirical research on efforts to promote the acquisition of tolerance and critical thinking skills may be found in the education literature. This literature generally focuses on classroom practices and implementation of curricula that promote these attributes, although some literature examines the school environment as a social setting in which children learn informally from their peers.

A key advantage of the classroom for promoting the acquisition of tolerance and critical thinking is that a teacher is present to facilitate discussion, ask key questions, and keep learning on track. Teachers play a critical role in promoting tolerance by teaching critical thinking skills and reinforcing their use in classroom discussions, production of oral and written reports, and in other classroom activities, such as science experiments (e.g., Willert and Willert, 2000). More generally, teachers can support the development and use of critical thinking skills by encouraging students to read deeply, to question, to engage in divergent thinking, to look for relationships among ideas, and to grapple with real-life issues (Carr, 1988).

The presence of a teacher who is engaged in these activities creates an environment that is consistent with Vygotsky's work discussed below in the section on developmental theories, which argues that scaffolding by an "expert" supports the acquisition of information by a "novice." The expert scaffolds the novice's understanding by breaking down information and providing support when the learner is having difficulty. A teacher is also able to recognize the "zone of proximal development" that applies either for the majority of the class or for each child (in more differentiated settings). Vygotsky argues that working within this zone maximizes learning because tasks within this zone present challenges that children generally find exciting because they are new; with help, the challenges are not too frustrating and the skill or material can be learned.

In searching for materials likely to promote tolerance and critical thinking, we decided that we had to assume that a person filling the teacher role would not be present as the child encounters the material, as discussed in Chapter Three. Parents may serve this function in some instances, but we could not assume that they would be present, willing, and able to take on these tasks. Increasingly, some media—for example, the Internet and television, are able, if they choose, to build in some interactivity (or pseudo-interactivity in the case of television) that supports learning; some Internet materials may even help with learning by including interactivity tailored to the abilities of a particular user.[4] Despite our assumption that a teacher or parent serving in that role would not be available to help the child understand the materials for which we would search, we concluded that a brief review of what happens in classrooms might provide us with clues as to the process by which tolerance can be taught. Thus, we conducted a literature review on classroom practices aimed at teaching tolerance and critical thinking. This review may be found in Appendix A.

Developmental Theories and Their Implications for Content That Promotes Tolerance and Critical Thinking

A number of psychological theories include concepts and processes that are particularly relevant to understanding children's development of tolerance and critical thinking skills. Below, we briefly describe three theories about how children learn and discuss the implications of each theory's concepts for how to select materials most likely to further the development of tolerance

---

[4] For example, during one children's TV show, characters stop and ask children questions, and time is allowed for the child viewers to answer. In another, the show was paused periodically to show a classroom of students and a teacher discussing the content. Actors sometimes model key behaviors.

and critical thinking. A table that summarizes key concepts associated with these theories may be found in Appendix B.

Social Learning Theory

Social learning theory (SLT) posits that much of children's learning occurs through observation of others and imitation of those models. SLT is nondevelopmental in that the mechanisms of learning—imitation and modeling—are assumed to be similar across children's development. However, the theory notes that what children are capable of imitating does differ by age. For example, young children may not be able to imitate behavioral sequences that are too complex for them to understand.

Numerous studies (see the discussion above and Bandura, 1977, for a review of some of this research) demonstrate that children imitate aggression and other behaviors that they observe. Imitation occurs when they observe behaviors in live action and even in more remote, animated form on television. As they age, children become increasingly sensitive to the reinforcement schedule that follows the behaviors they observe. For example, if they see a behavior that is rewarded they are more likely to imitate it.

Social learning theory suggests that it is important to pay attention to the behaviors portrayed in children's materials because they may be imitated by young readers and viewers. It is also important to pay attention to the way in which the consequences of the behavior are presented. If an individual is rewarded for enacting a behavior, this will increase the likelihood that a child who is interacting with the material will imitate that behavior. This latter point is particularly relevant in selecting content aimed at young children. Because young children tend to have fairly rigid moral frameworks with little room for ambiguity, successful content should punish bad behavior (or at least not lead to positive outcomes) and reward good behavior, which may include the protagonist being able to achieve his or her goals, receive recognition and praise for his behavior, etc. With older children, their greater ability to understand ambiguity may make simple rewards and punishments less believable and therefore may undermine the goal of a work.

Scaffolding and the Zone of Proximal Development

Scaffolding refers to the amount of support an "expert" on a topic (who could be an adult, such as a parent or teacher, but could also be another more-knowledgeable child or peer) provides to a "novice" in acquiring new information. The expert "scaffolds" the novice's understanding by breaking down information or tasks and providing support when the learner has difficulty. The effective expert diminishes his or her scaffolding/support of the novice as the novice acquires the skills and understanding necessary for the learning to occur. The *zone of proximal development* refers to a range of tasks that a child cannot yet complete on his or her own but is able to complete with help. The zone of proximal development is thought to be optimal for teaching because the new tasks represent a challenge, which makes the tasks appealing, but one that is still attainable. These concepts highlight learning that occurs through the social exchanges that children have with the people around them. These concepts, associated with Vygotsky (1978) have been highly influential in the fields of developmental psychology and education. They are relevant to the selection of persuasive materials for children because they suggest how concepts can most effectively be introduced to children of different ages. They suggest that media should challenge children but also break content down in a way that will help them process key messages. They also highlight the potential of newer technologies such as video games and especially the Internet because they can include interactive elements tailored to the abilities of a particular user.

Development of Cognitive and Moral Reasoning

Piaget (1983) and Kohlberg (1976, 1984) argue that children's cognitive and moral development unfolds in stages that are loosely tied to chronological age. Further, this development occurs in all children in a predictable way, so that certain basic concepts must be understood before the child can develop more sophisticated ones.[5] We relied on these stages to develop the criteria we used to identify optimal content and the ages for which content was most appropriate. Below we provide a summary of these stages. They are elaborated in Table B.1 in Appendix B.

Piaget described several stages of cognitive development. The relevant ones in this context are the preoperational, concrete operations, and formal operations stages, where "operations" refers to logical thought. In the *preoperational* stage, children are not able to take the perspectives of others—they view the world only through their own point of view. They are only able to focus their attention on a single aspect of what they are attending to at any given time (suggesting, in this context, that they would be able to attend to only a single storyline) and they often confuse cause and effect. Another relevant feature of this stage is that children focus on appearances, making it difficult for children to distinguish between what is real and what is fantasy in literature, television shows, and other media (Flavell, 1985). In the *concrete operations* stage, children's thinking becomes more logical, flexible, and organized about concrete information. It is during this stage that children become good at thinking about concrete things. By around ages 9–11, children are able to integrate multiple plot dimensions and can tell coherent stories with a main plot and several subplots. In the *formal operations* stage, abstract, scientific reasoning emerges. Children no longer require a concrete referent to evaluate the logic of a statement. Children begin to understand premises that contradict reality. In this stage adolescents can come up with new, more general logic rules through internal thought and reflection.

Kohlberg (1976, 1984) used Piaget's stages as a basis for mapping out six stages of development in children's moral reasoning that he grouped into three "periods." According to Kohlberg (1984), attaining higher levels of moral reasoning depends on children's abilities to engage in complex logical reasoning and perspective taking. The first is the *preconventional* period. Early in this period, moral judgments are largely based on a child's effort to avoid negative consequences (e.g., punishment) associated with breaking rules. Later in this period, the desire to satisfy personal needs typically determines moral choices. Throughout the period, children's judgments are based largely on egocentric motivations. During the *conventional* period, moral judgments are driven by efforts to comply with social standards. Early in this stage, maintaining the affection and approval of friends and relatives motivates good behavior. Later, a duty to uphold laws and rules for their own sake justifies moral conformity. During the *postconventional* stage, moral judgments are based on abstract, universal principles valid for all of humanity.

Piaget further argues that peers are particularly important in children's moral development. This is because children are more likely to question peers, a key aspect of learning, whereas they are more likely to accept without question the moral knowledge of authority

---

[5] The specific ages that Piaget and Kohlberg attached to particular stages have been disproved. However, the notion of stages and their sequencing remain hugely influential in the field of child development.

figures, such as adults. Thus, peer-to-peer relationships offer more opportunities for discussion and exchanges that lead to more sophisticated moral understanding than is typically the case in relationships between children and authority figures. Another key notion central to Piagetian theory is that children learn more when they are actively engaged in the learning process. In keeping with Piagetian theory, content from the Internet, where interactivity is much easier to build into games, lessons, and stories, is especially promising in this regard. Recent research suggests, for example, that people's opinions about race and other personal characteristics are shaped by adopting an avatar that is different on that characteristic, as discussed below.

Piaget's developmental stages and Vygotsky's notion of scaffolding both emphasize the role of social exchanges between experts and learners and between peers in the development of tolerance. These theories suggest that any media that promotes exchanges and interactions between the user and the material, particularly the protagonist, might be an effective way to facilitate learning. One intriguing line of research, which is being conducted by Jeremy Bailenson and his colleagues at Stanford University's Virtual Human Interaction Lab, underlines the importance of peer characteristics and the potential power of interactive media. Yee, Bailenson, and Ducheneaut (2009) found that in the course of playing interactive, virtual games, the physical characteristics of a player's avatar influence how young adults interact with other virtual characters. Perhaps more important, the characteristics of the avatar influenced players' social exchanges with others in the real world outside the game. For example, in one study, researchers manipulated the height of avatars. They found that people with taller avatars behaved more aggressively both within the virtual game and in a negotiation with another person in the lab following the game. They also looked at other avatar characteristics, such as physical attractiveness, and found similar spillover effects. This work suggests that exposing players to avatars with different characteristics—race, for example—could be a promising avenue for building empathy and exposing even young players to differences that may promote the development of tolerance.

Summary and Conclusions

Our review has clarified that tolerance and critical thinking skills can be taught. Such teaching presents children with people from different backgrounds who have different points of view, different needs, and different perceptions of a seemingly objective situation and encourages them to exercise mental agility, in terms of both defending positions taken and coming to conclusions about optimal solutions. There is also evidence that peer support for tolerance and critical thinking may be useful in encouraging the development and expression of these dispositions.

Our review of key theories helped us to determine the skills and abilities that children typically acquire as they develop in four key areas that we believe would be relevant to selecting works that effectively promote the development of tolerance and critical thinking: cognitive development, the ability to take the perspective of others, moral development, and emotional understanding. These lessons learned about the socialization of tolerance and critical thinking, along with our understanding of children's capacity in each of these areas as they mature, enabled us to develop criteria to identify and screen materials. The development and refinement of those criteria are discussed in Chapter Three.

Development of Screening Criteria

In this chapter, we discuss the translation of the theories and research presented in the previous chapter into the screening criteria we developed to identify materials that promote tolerance and critical thinking. We also describe the process we undertook to refine those criteria, including exploring their appropriateness in a non-Western setting and ensuring that coding was consistent across multiple raters.

As described in the previous chapter, we conducted extensive reviews of the literature on the development of tolerance and critical thinking. We also reviewed theory and research on the abilities that are important for developing tolerance and critical thinking. An example of such a skill is perspective taking. Very young children are unable to understand the fact that other people's views of the world may differ from their own. Yet, that ability may well be a prerequisite for tolerance. We then used the information we gathered to develop a set of criteria for coders to use in identifying promising materials and screening the collected materials to determine whether they convey the appropriate message and do so in a way that is consistent with the abilities of children at the ages to which the materials are targeted.

One of the challenges of identifying appropriate materials for children is that their abilities change dramatically over relatively short periods of time. Thus, what may be appropriate and appealing to a preschool-aged child is vastly different from what will engage and convey meaningful information to a child who is just a few years older. A judgment of age appropriateness must include a number of different developmental abilities. Examples of developmental abilities we considered include the extent to which the material requires perspective-taking abilities (younger children have greater difficulty in understanding the perspectives of others) and the complexity of moral understanding required (younger children tend to make moral attributions based on fear of reprisals rather than an understanding of rules). This added complexity to our task because, in addition to determining whether the material conveyed the right message, we also had to draw on theory and research to identify the sorts of messages children in a given age group could reasonably understand in the way that the author intended. The developmental abilities that we considered are described in greater detail below, as well as in the table of relevant skills by age in Appendix B. We also had to ensure that the other features of the material, e.g., font size, illustrations, length, were aligned with the complexity of the material and the age appropriateness of the message.

We were keenly aware that our review of literature and theory drew heavily on Western research and theories about child development, although we did include work from the region. To make sure that our categories were not inappropriately Western, we spent a great deal of time discussing them with staff members who had spent substantial time in different parts of the Middle East, including Lebanon, Jordan, Morocco, Qatar, and Egypt. In fact, three of the staff members grew up in the region and thus had been exposed as children to the types of materials we sought. To ensure that we included educators' perspectives as well, we identified three experts in education, two of whom work in the region, and asked them to review our criteria to make sure that we had incorporated any relevant differences between Western thinking and thinking in the Arab world in the development and use of the criteria.

Finally, because we felt that it was important to develop a coding scheme that could be applied consistently across coders, we took several steps to increase and assess intercoder rating consistency. While such intercoder reliability is a standard in psychological research, we thought it was a particularly important element to bring to the coding of materials that may be both subtle and charged. We developed and followed a training protocol (described below) that enabled us to both refine the coding categories and ensure that coders understood the meaning of the codes and how they applied to particular materials. As part of that process, we developed a detailed coding manual filled with examples that had been discussed and resolved to which coders could refer as they worked with new materials(see Appendix C for this manual).

This chapter is divided into the following five sections: (1) content codes derived from developmental theory and research designed to identify the appropriateness of the message conveyed; (2) the basis for identifying the appropriate age group for the material; (3) presentational factors considered in the selection of the materials; (4) description of the process we adopted for the development of the coding forms, including discussions with experts on education in the Arab world; and (5) coder training procedures aimed at ensuring that the coding system was applied with rigor and consistency. A more elaborate description of the rationale and definition for each code is provided in the coding manual (included in this report as Appendix C).

Content Codes Derived from Developmental Theories

The developmental theory that influenced us most in identifying the desired content of our materials was social learning theory (SLT). SLT highlights the extent to which people learn through observation and imitation. It also identifies conditions that aid in learning, e.g., any consequences that a model or protagonist experiences that children can observe influence the likelihood that children will imitate the protagonist. Drawing from SLT, we developed screening criteria that captured whether the material modeled diverse characters who got along with each other or who paid a price for not getting along. We included codes that captured whether the material explicitly modeled tolerance and critical thinking. We also identified characteristics of materials that incorporate social exchange highlighted by Vygotsky, Piaget, and others as important to children's socialization. Finally, we focused on identifying materials that should be within the zone of proximal development, using age as a proxy for children's abilities.

In keeping with these theories and the goals of our work, we included five types of codes described in more detail below: The coding categories were (1) diversity among the characters, (2) the quality of the relationships between the characters, (3) actions the characters directed toward one another, (4) the characters' ways of thinking, and (5) the emotional complexity exhibited by the characters.

Diversity. We coded for diversity among the characters portrayed in each of the works we reviewed. The aim of this code was to capture whether the material portrayed diverse or heterogeneous characters, dealt with diversity in more subtle ways, or made a broader argument about the value of diversity.[1] Given that the materials we reviewed were for children, we construed diversity broadly. For example, we coded diversity as being present in books targeted to young children when a variety of animal characters or characters of different colors were the main actors.

Relationship Codes. The aim of the relationship codes was to capture whether the nature of the characters' relationships conveyed a message of tolerance and acceptance. This might be done in several ways: showing characters relating positively or negatively to each other, then including some commentary on their relationship that reflects positively on a positive relationship and negatively on a negative one; or showing positive consequences from getting along or negative consequences from not getting along.

Action Codes. The aim of the action codes was to capture actions that highlighted tolerance; pro-social behaviors, such as kindness, sharing, and comforting of others; altruism (putting the needs of others before one's own); and other friendly overtures.

Thinking Codes. The aim of the thinking codes was to identify materials that support tolerance and critical thinking by portraying diverse ways of thinking. Our focus here was on situations that convey to children that there may be multiple ways to solve a problem and that different people can draw different conclusions from the same situation or information. Examples of situations where characters question authority were also coded here.

Emotional Complexity Codes. Emotional complexity was coded when the same character exhibited multiple emotions simultaneously or when different characters showed different emotional reactions to the same situation. Emotional complexity was coded because understanding that people can reasonably have different emotional reactions to the same situation contributes to the promotion of tolerance.

We also coded for whether the materials provided opportunities for active learning and scaffolding because SLT and other developmental theories posit, and the literature finds, that learning is facilitated when children are involved in the content. It is believed that active learning helps children focus and better absorb the material. To capture these constructs we included a set of codes that identified characteristics of the content that increase the likelihood that children will internalize and benefit from the positive messages that are conveyed in the material. This category is intended to capture the extent to which the potential viewer/user is drawn into the material and encouraged to make a response. Specifically, we coded whether the material provided opportunities for active learning (which could be as subtle as posing a question to the reader). We also coded whether the materials had any built-in exchanges to support or mimic interactivity. Finally, we coded whether efforts were made to provide scaffolding within the materials (e.g., breaking down complex content to make the message easier to understand).

As noted above, one of our challenges was that we needed to develop a basis for determining the age group for which each material was appropriate. Since development is complex and multidimensional, we needed to review a large body of literature to help our coders make the age category determination accurately and consistently. Coders also had to understand the importance of ensuring that the skills needed to fully and accurately understand the messages included in a particular material were likely to be found in children in the age range targeted by the material. In addition, the content and complexity of the messages and the presentational features of the material had to align with the skill set characteristics of the targeted age range.

---

[1] We included four types of diversity: character, self-perceived, allegorical, and Arab world–specific diversity. See the Coding Manual in Appendix C for more detail on each of these types of diversity.

Below we provide a summary of a number of key social, cognitive, moral and emotional abilities that change as children develop. Based on this information, coders determined whether the material appeared to be appropriate for children in their early years (ages 4–6), middle years (ages 7–10), or adolescents (ages 11–14). In cases where these different features did not align, e.g., the reading comprehension skills of the targeted cohort were insufficient to fully understand the work, the material was considered inappropriate for further screening.

Developmental Stages and Corresponding Abilities

To facilitate the identification of age-appropriate works for children, we mapped out key skills and abilities that children typically exhibit at different developmental stages. Specifically we focused on mapping the following abilities by age:

- *Cognitive development*: the transition from concrete to abstract thinking
- *Ability to take the perspective of others*: the shift from self-centered to other-oriented understanding and abilities
- *Moral development*: fear-based, approval-based, then rules-based compliance
- *Emotion and emotional understanding*: from limited emotional understanding to empathy.

These developmental abilities, linked to age ranges, are described in the table in Appendix B.

The above skills and abilities were highlighted because we considered them to be especially important in influencing the extent to which children would understand and benefit from the content of books, DVDs, or TV shows and other works designed to promote tolerance and critical thinking. It is important to note that the age groupings associated with each skill set should be treated cautiously. Individual children may attain these developmental skills at different ages, so the age groupings are intended as guidelines only. The material that is appropriate and effective for children of different ages varies significantly. Although research has confirmed the universality of many of these constructs (e.g., the stages of moral development outlined by Kohlberg), some of these constructs are also culturally dependent as their development depends on children's experiences and the values of their surrounding culture. It is for this reason that we located experts in different Arab cultures and drew on the expertise of the project team, the majority of whom have spent a significant amount of time living in the Middle East.

We considered several other abilities in developing the screening criteria. These include children's increasing linguistic and attentional abilities. For example, over the course of development the complexity of the language that children can understand (e.g., their vocabularies) increases dramatically. Overall, content that involves complex language structure and complicated words will not be appropriate for younger children.

Attentional abilities are also important in thinking about appropriate materials for children of different ages. The ability to sustain attention increases substantially with age. Children also become better at focusing on just those aspects of a more complex situation that are relevant for the task at hand. Older children are better at adapting attention to task requirements. Gains in attention are particularly marked in middle childhood (defined as ages 7–10).

The ability to understand humor is also something that develops with age. Younger children interpret stories and jokes quite literally and therefore are likely to miss the humor in a particular story. They have difficulty with sarcasm because they take statements quite literally.

While we tried to make sure that materials were not too advanced for a given age range, including material that is slightly beyond a child's abilities may not be a bad thing in all cases. Indeed, in keeping with Vygotsky's notion of the zone of proximal development, material that is just beyond what the child is capable of easily understanding is thought to be optimal because this material presents an attainable challenge if appropriate scaffolding is available. However, we did not assume in our selection criteria that such scaffolding would be provided by parents or teachers as children related to the materials we would select. For this reason, raters were asked to consider whether such supports are provided by the material itself; this kind of support may enable children to extract key messages on their own from the materials to which they are exposed. Without this support, messages may be missed or misunderstood.

Other Presentational Factors

In addition to the criteria developed based on theories and research in developmental psychology, we also identified "positive presentational elements" that we thought would increase children's engagement with the material. Specifically, we coded whether the material was visually engaging, whether the story, plot, and structure were appealing, and finally, whether the language used in the material would be interesting to children. While we felt that it was valuable to capture how engaging the materials were, it is important to recognize that this was by far the most subjective element of our coding scheme; it was difficult to do more than ask coders for their opinions on the attractiveness of the layout, how engaging illustrations were, and whether other production values, e.g., quality of paper and binding, increased or decreased the overall attractiveness of the material. Because these assessments were so subjective, these presentational elements were the only elements of the screening criteria that were scored on a 3-point scale, rather than coded as present or absent.

Development and Refining of the Codes

The two psychologists engaged in this work developed an initial set of codes and presented them to the Arabic-speaking staff who would be doing the coding. Coders, all of whom are fluent in Arabic and who had all spent significant amounts of time in Lebanon, Jordan, Morocco, Qatar, or Egypt, provided input about the relevance of our criteria in the Arab world, as well as raising questions about what the codes meant and what sorts of character actions and behaviors fit each one. Once we had a working draft of the criteria we had the coders test them by independently coding a small number of materials. Differences in their coding were resolved through group discussions, and modifications were made to clarify the coding criteria as needed. These modifications were noted in the coding manual that coders would use as they coded materials.

Once all identified issues had been resolved, we shared the draft criteria with three experts in education in the Arab world who had been identified by experts in this country and by RAND staff members, based on extensive contacts in the Middle East. In wide-ranging telephone discussions, we talked about the codes that were then part of the coding scheme, ideas about additional codes that might be needed to capture key ideas in Arab cultures, and a general sense of the issues that we were trying to address through the work. In general, there was consensus that children everywhere are much the same, although the social contexts in which they grow up may vary considerably. Said one expert, "There is not much difference between your kids and ours." The experts did say, however, that while children have the same emotions, norms about the expression of these emotions vary substantially between the West and the Arab world. One noted that it was important to include the concept of empathy in our coding because of its importance in Arab cultures; it was added. Another believed that the criteria made sense and strongly supported the importance of interactional opportunities. She noted that "when questions are posed in the story, children naturally pause and think." One expert expressed concerns that the codes at that point focused more on tolerance than on critical thinking; we talked about ways to include more focus on critical thinking in the codes. One approach on which we agreed was to code for the presence of supports for questioning imbedded in the story or added at some point; in the case of online media, there might be real opportunities for interaction.

Coder Training Procedures

Once changes had been made to the coding categories based on these discussions with experts, we held several more staff meetings during which we discussed the new and revised codes and how each of the coders had applied them independently to selected materials. At this point, we asked coders to examine more challenging materials about which we expected disagreements concerning appropriateness and other matters. After we had reconciled differences and noted the reconciliations in the codebook, we proceeded to test the reliability of each of our coders prior to beginning the formal coding process. Reliability testing involves having two or more raters assess the same material and statistically testing the consistency in their ratings. Using percentage agreement for individual codes and Kappa statistics for the overall coding system, we tested the consistency of each coder against a "gold standard" coder selected because of his clear grasp of the concepts we had included. With sufficient training, all coders were able to meet or exceed the minimum reliability criteria of 80 percent agreement or greater and a Kappa statistic of .60 or greater, indicating that they all were utilizing the coding system in a consistent way. It also suggests that future coders could, with sufficient training, reliably use the coding criteria to code new works for children.

The final coding form is presented in Appendix C along with the manual for use by the coders.

Conclusion

We developed a set of screening criteria based on our extensive review of the developmental psychology and social psychology literature and on key developmental theories. We engaged in a rigorous, iterative development process that drew from existing theory and research, and that included input from education experts in the Arab world and from our Arabic speaking coders. These efforts produced a set of screening criteria that coders could consistently apply to a wide range of materials developed for children of different ages. In Chapter Four, we describe the process of locating these materials and analyze key characteristics of the materials we collected and accepted into our repository. We also provide examples of several of the materials in our repository.

The Materials Search Process and Description of the Collection

This chapter describes how RAND conducted its search for Arabic language children's media and how those works were obtained. The collection is then broken down by a number of key variables, including media type, author nationality, reader age group, and the primary theme of the work. Following this broad overview of the materials reviewed, the chapter presents examples of these works for each age group included in our search. It concludes with an analysis of the specific strengths and weaknesses of the collection.

How the Search Was Structured

Arabic-speaking staff set out to find and review at least 100 Arabic-language materials that held some promise of meeting our goals of promoting tolerance and/or critical thinking. Once the materials had been found, staff would apply the screening criteria in a formal, consistent way. Those works that met the criteria would form a final repository of works that had been vetted by the team as consistent with the goals of promoting tolerance and critical thinking. To maximize the number of accepted materials, RAND staff prescreened well over 100 materials. The 104 materials that were ultimately reviewed and formally coded are referred to in this chapter as "the collection." The 68 materials that were accepted based on the screening process described in Chapter Three are referred to as the "final repository."

The team used a variety of methods to identify promising works for review. These included locating and reading book reviews and book summaries, author backgrounds, and publishing records, as well as locating any endorsements or associations with organizations committed to promoting tolerance and critical thinking among Arab youth. In other words, attempts were made to prescreen materials before they were collected and coded so as to maximize the proportion of materials that would meet screening criteria and be included in the final repository. To illustrate the selection process, we give examples below for each of the methods used.

Book reviews and book summaries. An example of material chosen on the basis of a book review is *The King of Things,* a novel about a young Egyptian boy who uses his wits to overcome bullying and who becomes the defender of objects (desks, chairs, etc.) that are defaced by students. An online review of the novel described the work this way, "The events of 'The King of Things' take place at a boarding school in Egypt. Its protagonist, Karim, who is twelve years old and whose parents have traveled to work abroad, is enrolled in the boarding school. [Karim] is a very sensitive and gentle boy who plays the harmonica and has special abilities that allow him to talk to inanimate objects around him like chairs, ceilings, and buildings. Karim faces bullying and favoritism from some of the students and the teachers at school although he overcomes this through tolerance, forgiveness, and productive dialog."[1] In this case, the review's mention of "tolerance, forgiveness, and productive dialog" was a clear signal that the material was reasonably likely to meet our screening criteria, and on this basis, the novel was purchased and formally coded.

Book summaries were also consulted when available, although it must be noted that these often consisted of just a few short sentences. Typical of what could be accessed online are the short blurbs put out by the Lebanese publishing house Asala that identify the main themes of its children's books in bullet point format. Despite the sparseness of the summaries, Asala's listing of themes, including "Coexistence and Acceptance of the Other,"[2] helped the coders to identify books likely to meet screening criteria.

Author backgrounds and publishing records. Another approach to identifying promising works was to identify authors whose previous writing and other activities suggested a commitment to the values (tolerance and critical thinking) that our work was seeking to support through the identification of appropriate materials. For example, the Syrian writer, Ghālīyah Khūjah, was identified as an author whose works merited consideration because she was winner of the 1997 prize in children's literature awarded by Shaikhah Fā□imah al-Nahīyān and is both a universal peace ambassador and an ambassador to the Poets of the World organization. Just as author background factored in the selection process, so too did authors' publishing records. So, for example, the coding team reviewed additional works from authors of publications that had already met screening criteria. For example, in the case of Taghrīd ʿĀrif al-Najjār, a Jordanian writer who authored four materials in our collection, the fact that the first story written by Ms. al-Najjār that the team reviewed, "The Ogre," strongly promoted a message of tolerance and critical thinking led to the purchase and review of some of her other works—*When the Door Was Knocked, Don't Worry Dad*, and *The Story of a Boy Named Fayez*.

Endorsements by or associations with like-minded organizations. A final approach to selecting materials for screening was to collect works that were either sponsored or endorsed by organizations associated with tolerance and critical thinking. For example, the fact that Khālid Jumʿah's story *Sheep Don't Eat Cats* was sponsored by UNESCO and the Tamer Institute for Community Education—a local Palestinian organization committed to promoting tolerance—gave the team confidence that the material had a high likelihood of meeting screening criteria. In addition to UNESCO and the Tamer Institute, we selected materials for review that were either sponsored or endorsed by the Goethe Institute, the International Labor Organization, and the International Committee of the Red Cross.

How the Materials Were Collected

Materials were collected through a variety of means, including the purchase of hard copies through online book sellers; the purchase of materials in the course of visits to Jordan, Lebanon, and Syria;[3] accessing of materials freely available on the Web; and directly contacting

---

[1]   Moheet.com, "*The King of Things*, the first Egyptian novel for children, is in its second edition," [In Arabic], December 22, 2007.

[2]   This was one of three themes listed for the children's book *The Story of Two Trees*.

[3]   These visits were not part of structured fieldwork. Rather, team members purchased materials in the course of personal visits to the region.

Figure 4.1
Method of Collection (all 104 works reviewed)

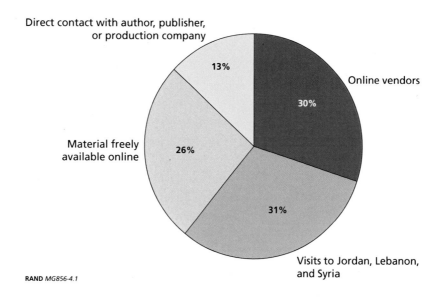

authors, publishers, or production companies in instances where materials were not available for purchase through vendors. A breakdown of how the collection was obtained is provided in Figure 4.1.

As illustrated in Figure 4.1, the three most common methods of collection were the purchase of books during visits to the region, the purchase of books through online vendors like *Maktabat Nīl wa Fūrāt* (The Nile and Euphrates Bookstore) and *Adab wa Fann* (Literature and Art),[4] and accessing materials freely available online.[5] In addition, a smaller but still significant number of materials (13 percent) were collected by contacting authors, publishers, or production companies to track down works not available through other means.

Additional Considerations That Informed the Search

In the course of identifying and collecting promising materials, the team also sought balance in the collection at three different levels. First, the collection team made sure that all subregions that make up the Arab world (North Africa, the Levant, and the Arab Gulf countries[6]) were represented in the catalog. Second, balance was sought in the number of materials that

---

[4] These online vendors are the closest thing the Arab World has to Amazon.com. Their websites are found at http://www.neelwafurat.com/ and http://www.adabwafan.com/. Most Arab publishers do not sell their materials directly to customers online; rather, they rely on large vendors like *Maktabat Nīl wa Fūrāt*, as well as local book stores that often carry their name.

[5] Personal websites of authors like Khālid Jumʿah (http://www.khaledjuma.com/) were one source of online content. Other sources of online materials were sites such as al-Hakawati (http://www.al-hakawati.net/) that include broader collections of works. Finally, the Alexandria Library in Egypt has made much of its collection available online at http://www.bibalex.org/English/index.aspx.

[6] In this study, North Africa is defined as Morocco, Algeria, Tunisia, Libya, Egypt, and the Sudan; the Levant is defined as Jordan, Lebanon, Palestine, and Syria; the Arab Gulf countries are Bahrain, Iraq, Kuwait, Oman, Qatar, Saudi Arabia, the UAE, and Yemen.

promoted tolerance versus those that promoted critical thinking. Finally, efforts were made to have equal representation of materials targeting each of the three age groups (4–6 years old, 7–10 years old, and 11–14 years old). This meant that we made a special effort to find North African and Arab Gulf materials because Levantine materials had dominated our early search efforts. Materials that supported tolerance were far more plentiful than those that portrayed critical thinking; finding the latter took extra effort. This does not mean that the catalog achieved perfect balance; despite our best efforts, it is still weighted toward materials from Levantine authors, just as there are more works that focus on tolerance than on critical thinking. However, readers should keep in mind that the catalog is more balanced than a random sample of materials would be. Without these efforts, the assembled materials would have been very heavily weighted toward Levantine authors and the promotion of tolerance rather than critical thinking. As for the target age group, the least well-represented cohort was 4–6-year-olds. This is best explained by the fact that while Arabic language media targeting these youngest children is plentiful, the materials tend to focus on teaching the alphabet or other simple themes that do not lend themselves well to conveying the more complex concepts of tolerance and critical thinking.

Search Results[7]

In total, the team collected and reviewed 104 materials drawn from different media. The materials encompass short stories, cartoons, novels, magazines and comic books, educational materials, and poetry. A breakdown of the collection by media type is provided in Figure 4.2.

Figure 4.2
Materials by Media Type (all 104 works reviewed)

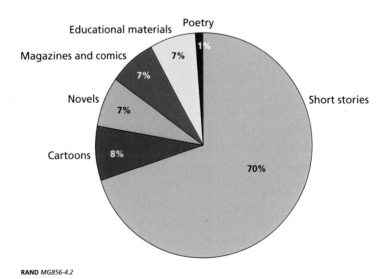

---

[7] The following data capture the characteristics of the collection, i.e., the 104 materials that were collected and reviewed by the Arabic-speaking team. The same analysis was conducted on the smaller set of 68 materials that were found to have met the project criteria and comprise the final repository. Although we examined both the collection and the repository on several key characteristics including media type, author nationality, and age cohort, it was only in media type that we found a significant difference between the characteristics of the collection and the final repository. Consequently, we show data for both the collection and the repository for that characteristic only.

As illustrated in Figure 4.2, the bulk of the collection is made up of short stories. Simply put, this is a reflection of the limited availability of the other types of media. Specifically, there are very few indigenously produced cartoons in the Arab world—and fewer still promoting the values on which we focused. Cartoons shown in the Arab world are generally dubbed versions of content created in the West and thus were not eligible for inclusion in our collection. On the other hand, the relatively small proportion of novels can be attributed to the fact that we were searching for materials for children no older than age 14. Thus, the literature collected tended to be in the form of short stories aimed at children who have yet to acquire the reading and attentional skills necessary to tackle full-length novels. As illustrated in Figure 4.3, this weighting becomes even more pronounced when the analysis is restricted to the 68 accepted works rather than the entire 104 materials reviewed. Thus, short stories were not only easier to find, they also evidenced a greater probability of meeting the screening criteria.

Our analysis of the origin of the materials revealed a strong Levantine bias. As shown in Figure 4.4, more than half (52 percent) of the materials collected were authored or produced in the four countries of the Levant—Jordan, Lebanon, Palestine, and Syria—despite strong efforts to ensure geographic diversity. North Africa was the origin of 30 percent of the materials, followed by the Arab Gulf states, which contributed 9 percent of the collection that we subsequently screened. Finally, the author or producer's nationality could not be determined for 9 percent of the materials.

The preponderance of materials from the Levant can be attributed to three primary factors. First, Lebanon remains the dominant player in Arabic language publishing. This means that Levantine authors have more opportunities to bring their work to print. Second, the Levantine states are quite diverse. For example, Lebanon has significant populations of Christian, Druze, and Shi'a Muslims. Palestine and Syria also boast large Christian populations, and the latter also has a significant Kurdish minority. Finally, there are small Christian and Circassian populations in Jordan. This religious and ethnic diversity provides both the context and impetus for Levantine authors to introduce the theme of tolerance into their work. Finally,

Figure 4.3
Materials by Media Type (68 accepted works only)

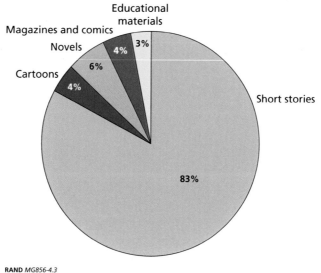

Figure 4.4
Breakdown by Author Nationality (all 104 works reviewed)

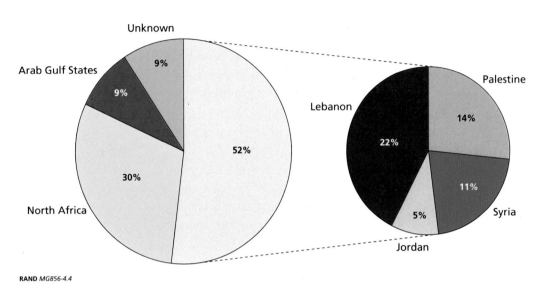

the countries of the Levant generally enjoy more social freedoms than their Gulf counterparts, allowing the former greater latitude in promoting such values as critical thinking and the acceptance of differences.

While we attempted to balance materials across the three age groupings, Figure 4.5 illustrates a slight weighting of the collection toward children ages 7–10. However, there is significant representation of the other two age cohorts.

In examining materials to be considered for the collection, we found that, in general, tolerance is a much more common theme in Arabic language children's media than critical thinking; this is reflected in the makeup of the collection. The screening criteria employed in the coding of materials provided numerous ways to record tolerance, although the most obvi-

Figure 4.5
Breakdown by Age Cohort (all 104 works reviewed)

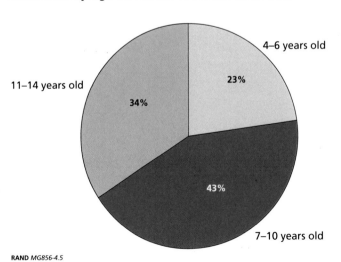

ous and direct was the code: "At least one character acts in a tolerant or pro-social way." Of the 104 materials reviewed, 62 percent met this criterion. Moreover, within this set of materials, tolerance was often the *central* theme in the work, with the message communicated directly (i.e., employing scaffolding) or through metaphor. Critical thinking was most directly measured using three coding criteria: "Different ways to think or solve a problem are discussed or shown," "Question rules, authority or societal assumptions while thinking or problem solving," and "Draw different conclusions from the same information." In total, 53 percent of materials met at least one of these three criteria, although it must be recalled that extra effort was made in the search process to locate materials with critical thinking themes. In addition, critical thinking was frequently a *secondary* rather than a primary theme in these works.

The limited availability of Arabic language children's media promoting critical thinking can be explained by three main factors. The first is that the skills needed to think critically do not develop until children reach the oldest of the age groups considered in this study, so it is not surprising that it was rare to encounter the theme in materials aimed at the 4–6 and 7–10 cohorts. Second, critical thinking tends to be a prominent theme of educational materials (see Appendix A); this category comprised a relatively small share (7 percent) of our collection. Finally, critical thinking is a particularly difficult message to integrate into children's media given that a dominant theme of the works we collected, particularly those written for the youngest children, is actually to reinforce compliant behaviors such as obeying parents. This focus on compliance is consistent with a strong emphasis on such messages in materials produced in the region for young children (e.g., UNDP, 2003). Below, we present descriptions of several works that met our criteria. One work for each of the study age groups is described in some detail.

Example from the Collection for Children Ages 4–6

Title: *Sheep Don't Eat Cats*   **Title (Arabic):** الخراف لا تأكل القطط

Author: Khālid Jum'ah   **Author (Arabic):** خالد جمعة

Summary: This is the story of a family of cats that are frightened by their new neighbors—a family of sheep. The father of the cat family is particularly anxious and forbids any intermingling with the sheep. However, the curiosity of the youngest cat leads to an exchange with the sheep that confirms that the sheep mean no harm to the cats. The moral of the story is not to demonize "the other" and that young people should move beyond the fears and stereotypes of their parents' generation.

Author Background: A Palestinian poet and writer of children's stories, Khālid Jum'ah lives in Rafah (Gaza). He is a frequent collaborator with both Tamer Institute and various UN organizations including UNESCO and UNRWA.

Values Communicated: Acceptance of diversity, positive relationships, tolerant or pro-social behavior, emotional complexity

Age Cohort: 4–6 years   **Aimed at Specific Gender:** No, the material is appropriate for both boys and girls.

Publisher and Date of Publication: Tamer Institute for Community Education (2005)

Media Type: Book   **ISBN:** 9950326230

Example from the Collection for Children Ages 7–10

Title: *The Story of a Boy Named Fayez*   **Title (Arabic):** قصة ولد اسمه فايز

Author: Taghrīd ʿĀrif al-Najjār   **Author (Arabic):** تغريد عارف النجار

Summary: Fayez is a young boy who is preoccupied with his thoughts, earning him a reputation as a daydreamer. The other kids poke fun at him since this leads him to do things like wear two different shoes. In another instance, Fayez is caught by his teacher staring out the window at clouds whose shapes remind him of animals. Although Fayez is creative, he does not get good evaluations in art class because the instructor asks the students to do things by rote like reproducing a flower vase. Fayez makes a vase, but takes artistic license to change its form, which does not please the instructor.

Then, during summer vacation, his father tries to teach him the trade of stone masonry. Fayez catches on but quickly gets bored by the repetitive nature of the work. One day, while toiling at the workshop with his father, Fayez imagines a creature that takes him to a dream world where he ends up playing and dancing with the different stones. This daydream convinces Fayez that carving rocks isn't boring, and he throws himself into the work, hoping that the creature that visited him will return. Soon Fayez is experimenting and carving rocks into different shapes (fish, horses, cars, plants, etc.). This angers his father, who considers it a waste of time. However, while he is reprimanding Fayez, the owner of the workshop (a woman) comes by, and she is impressed by Fayez's work. She buys some of his pieces and asks Fayez's father if the boy may begin taking art classes at the institute she runs.

The father ultimately agrees, and Fayez loves the institute where he learns different arts and becomes the star pupil. At the end of the summer, Fayez wins first place in an art exhibition, leading to an article about him in the newspaper and an interview on TV. He also becomes popular at school, where the students ask for his help with art and he earns the nickname, "Fayez the Artist."

Author Background: Taghrīd ʿĀrif al-Najjār is a Jordanian author who has published over 30 illustrated children's books, including *The Ogre*, which also appeared as a segment on Arabic-language Sesame Street. The author holds a degree in English literature and certificates in education and psychology from the American University in Beirut. Before becoming a writer and publisher, she worked for several years as an educator. She founded al-Salwa Publishing House in 1995.

Values Communicated: Acceptance of diversity, positive relationships, tolerant or pro-social behavior, critical thinking

Age Cohort: 7–10 years   **Aimed at Specific Gender:** No, the material is appropriate for both boys and girls although the story's protagonist is a boy.

Publisher and Date of Publication: Al-Salwa Publishing House (2008)

Media Type: Book   **ISBN:** 9789957040437

Example from the Collection for Children Ages 11–14

Title: *And on That Night*   **Title (Arabic):**   و في تلك الليلة

Author: Samīr Mālṭī   **Author (Arabic):** سمير مالطي

Summary: This is a story about the sons (Walid and Samir) of the shaikhs of two tribes that share the same oasis. The oasis has abundant water, date trees, and pasture for livestock, and Walid and Samir become the best of friends. However, competition between the tribes over water leads to fighting, with the conflict escalating to the point that tribe members are killed in clashes over access to it. This leads the shaikhs of the two tribes to cover up the water source—in order to prevent further conflict—and to cut off contact between the two tribes. Walid's father warns him against meeting Samir. However, after three days apart, Walid and Samir reunite under the date tree where they had always passed their time. Life becomes very difficult for the tribes because of the water conflict. Nevertheless, two years pass without any reconciliation. Then, winter comes and brings less rain than expected, worsening the situation until both shaikhs are on the verge of moving their tribes out of the oasis. Walid and Samir are unwilling to be split apart, and one night they decide to take it upon themselves to uncover the water source. When they do this, the water gushes forth, awakening the tribe members. The shaikhs of the two tribes take the opportunity to reconcile and the book ends with both tribes celebrating the prospects of a new, conflict-free life in the oasis. Finally, the skies open and it begins to pour rain, symbolizing God rewarding the reconciliation.

Author Background: Unknown

Values Communicated: Acceptance of diversity, positive relationships, tolerant or pro-social behavior, critical thinking, emotional complexity

Age Cohort: 11–14 years   **Aimed at Specific Gender:** No, the material is appropriate for both boys and girls although the main characters in the story are two boys and their fathers.

Publisher and Date of Publication: Asala Publishing (2009)

Media Type: Book   **ISBN:** 9789953537337

Rejected Works

Despite careful prescreening of materials through the methods described above, not all of the works collected met screening criteria. Prescreening was not 100 percent effective because book reviews and book summaries were often very short and could be misleading, just as authors' backgrounds and past publishing records were not always an accurate indicator of the degree to which a given work conveyed messages that aligned with our screening criteria. In total, 68 works, or roughly two-thirds of the collection, were accepted. These 68 works comprise the final repository. The remaining 36 works were generally rejected because of insufficient attention to the values the materials were selected to promote. It should be noted that most of the rejected materials were not promoting intolerance or encouraging blind obedience to norms or rules; the materials simply did not explicitly promote tolerance or critical thinking. For example, in the entertaining and attractively illustrated book, *I Didn't Mean To,* a young girl gets herself into trouble by stopping up the sink with clay, locking the door to her room and then misplacing the key, getting gum stuck in her hair, etc. The story ends with the girl noting that in the future she will consider the consequences before acting. Of course, there is nothing unsettling about the material and in fact it does a good job of teaching a valuable lesson: deliberateness and responsibility. However, the material was rejected given that it promotes neither of the two values—tolerance and critical thinking—that were the focus of this work.

Materials were also disqualified for several other reasons. For example, works were rejected if they promoted intergroup understanding at the expense of another group. For example, one rejected book encouraged unity between Christian and Muslim Palestinians in order to unite against Israeli occupation.[8] Another rejection criterion concerned the outcome of the critical thinking process portrayed. For example, one story was rejected because its protagonist opposed rules that limited fasting during Ramadan to older children. The material was judged to be antithetical to our goals because the story promoted greater religious piety than the societal norm.[9]

Analysis of the Collection: Strengths

The process of collecting and then coding over 100 examples of Arabic language children's media revealed a number of positive findings. Perhaps the most significant is that there exists a large body of children's literature indigenous to the region that promotes tolerance, coexistence, and respect for the "other." Jawdat 'Īd (Palestinian), Khālid Jum'ah (Palestinian), 'Āyadah Nu'mān (Lebanese), Hanādī Dīyyah (Lebanese), and Taghrīd 'Ārif al-Najjār (Jordanian) have all authored multiple children's stories that are well-written, entertaining, and which promote tolerance as a central theme. This finding is heartening for those seeking to promote tolerance in the Arab world, although it must be balanced against the limited availability of these works outside of well-to-do commercial districts in the Levant (e.g., al-Hamra neighborhood in Beirut) and for the small share of parents in the region who purchase books online.

A second finding that augurs well for the promotion of tolerance and critical thinking is the strong sense of mission among many of the creators of these works. The efforts of a number of these authors, who engage in a range of activities that go well beyond producing content, help to increase the audience for works that often are little-known and poorly distributed. A deep commitment to promoting tolerance and critical thinking among young people can be observed in authors like □āriq 'Abd al-Bārī (Egyptian) and □alā□ al-Dīn al-□amādī (Tunisian) who self-publish in order to make their works available and increase their reach. A strong sense of mission may also be observed in authors like Jawdat 'Īd and Khālid Jum'ah, both of whom have made a number of their materials freely available online to increase their accessiblity. Authors' commitment to making a difference is also evident in several authors' collaborations with local and international organizations and in the efforts of those like Taghrīd 'Ārif al-Najjār, who not only writes children's stories but also engages in teacher training, thereby helping educators become better advocates for these values.

---

[8] Najlā' Nasīr Bashūr, *Sha'nūnat al-'Īd,* ("Palm Sunday"), Beirut: Mu'sasat Tāla: 2004.

[9] Hibah al-'Awīnī, *Lastu Saghīran 'alá al-Siyām* ("I'm Not too Young to Fast"), Malayin, Lebanon: Dar al-'Ilm lilmalayin: 2007.

RAND's research also revealed a number of important "firsts" in the region in the effort to convey messages of tolerance and critical thinking. Perhaps the most important was the creation in 2007 of the first three-dimensional cartoon from the region,[10] *Frīj* or "Neighborhood" in Gulf dialect, which is set in Dubai and focuses on four female characters who try to reconcile the social changes brought about by modernization with traditional values. And while this cartoon was ultimately rejected based on the tendency of the characters to reconcile these differences in favor of conservative values, other three-dimensional cartoons created since, such as the Egyptian show *Karākīb* (the name of a fictional planet), have employed the technology to encourage tolerance and critical thinking. The high production value of these cartoons is noteworthy; locally produced cartoons tend to have poor production values and do not match the excitement of dubbed Western cartoons. The production of more high-quality local programs such as these represents a promising vehicle for reaching Arabic-speaking children, given the high penetration of satellite television programming in the region.

Another important first is the emergence of Arabic language novels specifically aimed at "tweens," children who are generally between the ages of 10 and 13. Just as in the West, this age group has long had to cope with materials whose content and storylines are too simplistic for their emotional development or that speak to the emotional issues they confront but may not be accessible given their levels of reading comprehension. However, in 2006, the Egyptian writer □āriq 'Abd al-Bārī penned what he describes as "the first full length Egyptian literary novel for children and youth."[11] The book, which features a 12-year-old protagonist and bears similarities to the Harry Potter series, is clearly aimed at the underserved "tween" cohort. The fact that the novel became a phenomenon in Egypt—necessitating a second print run less than a year after it was released—illustrates the pent-up demand in the market for material written specifically for this age group.

RAND's search also turned up a number of works that take on taboo or otherwise sensitive subjects, a fact that points to some sense among authors of a more open publishing space, particularly in Lebanon. Two notable books in this regard are *I Live…* by Hanādī Dīyyah and *A Street Kid* by Fayrūz al-Ba'lbakkī. *I Live* is narrated by a child who lives with both of his divorced parents. While divorce is not uncommon in the region, the arrangement portrayed in the book—shared custody and continued contact and cooperation between the two parents for the sake of the child—describes a family situation that differs substantially from the social norm. The second book, *A Street Kid,* describes the experience of a teenage boy who suffers from domestic abuse at the hands of his alcoholic father. Not only does the background of the story shed light on a little-talked-about social problem, but the message of the book—that youth should not passively obey authority and should know their legal rights—challenges the prevailing norm of compliant behavior. Not coincidentally, both authors are Lebanese and the books were printed and distributed by Lebanese publishing houses.

---

[10] "MBC produces Tash Cartoon and four other series from Dubai Satellite TV," *Asharq al-Awsat* newspaper, October 27, 2006 [In Arabic].

[11] Ṭāriq 'Abd al-Bārī, *Malik al-Ashīyā'* ("The King of Things"), Self-published, 2006.

Analysis of the Collection: Weaknesses

Although RAND's collection of Arabic language children's literature reveals a number of heartening trends, it also suggests some weaknesses. The first and most obvious is the often poor production quality of books published in the region. In the case of one book, pages 37–48 were mistakenly printed in place of pages 73–84, effectively creating a 12-page gap in the novel. Many of the books suffered from poor quality paper and printing that made them difficult to read. Other books lacked illustrations; what illustrations did exist were unattractive and not likely to engage young readers. Online content was beset by its own problems; there were numerous broken links, examples of authors posting text but not illustrations, or text abruptly cutting off before the end of the story. Poor production quality is probably best explained by two factors. First, the emphasis on keeping books affordable, particularly in poorer countries like Egypt, leads to the use of cheap materials. And second, poor presentation of online content suggests that authors are forced to rely on a do-it-yourself approach to posting content rather than having dedicated IT support from a publisher.

Alongside the weaknesses in production quality were deficiencies in content. Some of the materials collected were characterized by overly formulaic plots or tired metaphors. The use, for example, of a rainbow to represent diversity was so common that the search team actually stopped accepting these types of works to avoid redundancy. In other cases, the writing itself was not engaging or, in the case of folk tales, used a stilted form of classical Arabic unlikely to appeal to today's generation of children.

Finally, as noted earlier, there is an acute shortage of indigenously produced children's television programming. The cartoons shown in the region are still predominately dubbed versions of materials created in the West. There are some positive developments on this front, with the Jordanian production *Ben and Izzy* and the Egyptian cartoon *Karākīb* meriting particular attention. However, the high production costs associated with this type of medium limit the opportunities for local writers, artists, and producers to create original Arabic language content. This gap is particularly significant given the high penetration of satellite TV in the region and its potential to reach audiences in areas where illiteracy remains high. In these areas, there may not be a strong tradition of pleasure reading, and Internet connectivity is generally low.

Conclusion

We utilized a variety of methods to prescreen materials before they were purchased and coded. These methods included using book reviews and summaries, author backgrounds and publishing records, and any sponsorship or association with international organizations as indicators of promising materials for review. This process contributed to a high rate of acceptance of the works we collected, with two-thirds of the works reviewed ultimately meeting screening criteria for inclusion in the final repository. All of these accepted works either promote tolerance, critical thinking, or both. Most of the rejected materials did not promote intolerance; they simply paid insufficient attention to the core values that these materials were selected to promote. For example, materials were rejected that encouraged children to pick up after themselves or obey their parents if those messages were not coupled with specific attention to developing tolerance and critical thinking.

Although different types of media were considered in the collection process, the final catalog is strongly weighted toward print material, and specifically short stories. This is due to a shortage of locally produced television programming (e.g., cartoons) and the fact that other literary forms (e.g., novels) are beyond the reading comprehension of the youngest age group included in the study. The catalog is also weighted toward materials authored in the Levant, although there is representation from the Arab Gulf and North African countries as well. The preponderance of literature from the Levant can be traced to the importance of Lebanon to Arab publishing, the religious diversity of the subregion, and a freer environment for the public discussion of sensitive topics.

The process of collecting and reviewing these materials revealed a number of positive trends. Most importantly, the catalog confirms that there is actually a good deal of children's literature written in Arabic promoting tolerance and respect for the "other." Moreover, many of the creators go well beyond simply producing these works. Based on a strong sense of the importance of the societal values they promote in their written works, some of these authors conduct teacher training on how best to use these materials and team up with international organizations to spread their message. However, the potential impact of their work often is mitigated by a number of weaknesses in the accepted materials. Specifically, some materials suffer from low production values and formulaic content. Finally, a shortage of locally produced cartoons removes an important means of connecting to publics who may have barriers to finding and relating to print materials. This medium has the potential to reach far larger audiences than print material or online content.

CHAPTER FIVE

Summary and Future Directions

This study was premised on a widely accepted sense both inside and outside the Arab world that reform is necessary to further human development in the region. A critical component of reform is the building of a knowledge society. A key aspect of a knowledge society is a well-educated citizenry that is open to new ideas and the production of local knowledge through the use of its capacity for critical thinking and its tolerance of other views.

One approach to promoting these goals is to capitalize on the rich cultural resources already being produced in the Arabic language to promote new ideas and support the development of critical thinking. The work described in this report is part of a broader effort to identify and disseminate materials whose messages encourage tolerance and support the development and use of critical thinking skills.

Expanding the ranks of individuals who are open to considering and understanding others' beliefs and are able to analyze information and come up with new ideas and local knowledge is key to building a knowledge society. Our work, based on research and theory in developmental and social psychology, assumes that inculcating these ways of thinking early on will support these goals. Children model what they see portrayed in books, films, and cartoons. How the heroes of these stories fare has a strong impact on the extent to which their behaviors will be copied and internalized by children.

Our efforts to find and screen works for children between the ages of 4 and 14 that promote tolerance and critical thinking revealed the presence of a significant body of indigenous children's literature that promotes these values. Our search produced more works that focus on diversity and tolerance than on critical thinking, not surprising given that promoting critical thinking is a much more cognitively complex task that is difficult to undertake in works for the younger children in our age range. And although some of the works lacked high production values or were formulaic in their content, we found a number of materials that employed attractive characters and interesting plots to convey the value of diversity and the importance of thinking for oneself. However, these works have both geographical and cultural limitations. Most may be found largely in well-to-do commercial districts in the Levant (e.g., the al-Hamra neighborhood in Beirut); they are easily accessible outside this area only to the small share of parents in the region who purchase books online.[1] Moreover, some of these works reflect secular values, e.g., girls wearing skirts and limited references to piety, or portray situations that would only resonate with elites, e.g., how to treat one's domestic workers or interact

---

[1] Internet connectivity varies greatly within the region, with some of the wealthier Persian Gulf states boasting relatively high penetration rates (in Kuwait, Qatar, and the UAE, more than one in four residents are Internet users) and very low penetration in other states, particularly those with poorer, rural populations, such as Yemen and Sudan, where fewer than one in ten residents are Internet users. (Statistics are drawn from the 2009 Arab Human Development Report.)

with foreigners while traveling abroad. Although these materials model tolerance and critical thinking, they may not be appealing or even appropriate in the more conservative countries of the region, just as they are unlikely to resonate among poorer segments of the population who cannot identify with the characters' lives.

Many of these tolerance-promoting works are produced by authors with a strong commitment to these values. Some self-publish in order to make their work available or to increase the reach of their work. Others have made a number of their materials freely available online. Still others collaborate with local and international organizations; one author trains teachers to become better advocates for these values.

RAND's work also revealed important developments in the region that are expanding the reach of media that might convey messages of tolerance and critical thinking. Perhaps the most important development was the creation in 2007 of the first three-dimensional cartoon from the region.[2] Frīj ("Neighborhood" in Gulf dialect) is set in Dubai and focuses on four female characters who try to reconcile the social changes brought about by modernization with traditional values. While this cartoon was ultimately rejected from our final repository because its characters reconcile these differences in favor of conservative values, other three-dimensional cartoons created since, like the Egyptian show *Karākīb* (the name of a fictional planet), have employed this technology to encourage tolerance and critical thinking. The high production value of these cartoons and the high penetration of satellite television programming in the region make these shows a promising vehicle for reaching Arab children with these messages.

Another important recent development is the emergence of Arabic language novels specifically aimed at "tweens." This age group has long had to cope with a paucity of appropriate materials that are sophisticated enough to be appealing but also accessible in light of often limited reading comprehension skills. In 2006, the first full-length Egyptian literary novel for children and youth, □āriq 'Abd al-Bārī's *The King of Things,* was published. The book, which features a 12-year-old protagonist and bears similarities to the Harry Potter series, is clearly aimed at the "tween" cohort. The novel became a phenomenon in Egypt—necessitating a second print run less than a year after it was released. This suggests a pent-up demand for compelling material written specifically for this age group.

RAND's search also turned up a number of works for young people that deal with taboo or otherwise sensitive subjects, a fact that points to a freer publishing space, particularly in Lebanon. One notable Lebanese book deals with shared custody and cooperation among divorced parents on behalf of their son, a situation that differs substantially from the typical post-divorce arrangement in the region. A second Lebanese book describes the experience of a teenage boy who suffers from domestic abuse at the hands of his alcoholic father. Not only does the story shed light on a little-talked-about social problem, but the message of the book—that youth should know their legal rights and not passively obey authority—challenges the prevailing norm of compliant behavior that we found in many of the books we examined that were directed at younger children.

Despite these encouraging signs, we encountered significant limitations in the supply of children's materials. In poorer Arab countries, serious constraints on the price that parents can or will pay for children's materials contribute to such poor production quality that the appeal of these materials is limited. These quality defects are often accompanied by deficiencies in

---

2   See "MBC produces Tash Cartoon and four other series from Dubai Satellite TV."

content: formulaic plots often employ tired metaphors such as rainbows to convey diversity. Some of the writing itself is not engaging; a number of folk tales employed a stilted form of classical Arabic unlikely to appeal to today's generation of children.

There is an acute shortage of indigenously produced children's television programming; we know, because we looked diligently for it. Indeed, our final catalog is strongly weighted toward print material, and specifically short stories, because of the lack of such programs. The cartoons shown in the region are still predominately dubbed versions of materials created in the West; locally developed programs with far less dynamic and modern production values cannot compete. The Jordanian production *Ben and Izzy* and the Egyptian cartoon *Karākīb* are notable exceptions. But the high production costs associated with this type of media limit opportunities for local writers, artists, and producers to create original Arabic language content; this is particularly unfortunate because high satellite penetration potentially could bring these programs into many homes. In a region with high illiteracy, little tradition of pleasure reading, and low levels of Internet connectivity, such programs and their messages could have powerful effects. However, efforts to encourage more such programming may be fruitless in the current context because of severe problems with copyrighting. Those who might invest in such programming understand that there are few profits to be made because pirating of material is so widespread in the region; virtually everyone buys pirated DVDs.

We took considerable care to select materials that appeared, based on an assessment of available information, to hold promise of meeting screening criteria. Thus it is not surprising that most of the collected materials that were ultimately rejected did not promote intolerance or reject analytic thought; rather, they simply paid insufficient attention to the core values they were being selected to promote. For example, a number of materials were rejected whose message was to obey and comply; they encouraged children to pick up after themselves or obey their parents and provided limited if any support for developing tolerance and critical thinking.

Not surprisingly, our final catalog is weighted toward materials authored in the Levant, although there is representation from the Arab Gulf and North African countries as well. The preponderance of literature from the Levant can be traced to the importance of Lebanon to Arabic publishing. The religious diversity of that subregion naturally leads to stories of diversity and a freer environment for the public discussion of sensitive topics.

A number of barriers exist to increasing both the supply and quality of these materials. Earlier RAND work that focused on the identification of Arabic-language adult materials with similar goals identified a number of barriers to production, dissemination, and use of these materials. These barriers included few bookstores, few public libraries, the banning of more liberal books while subsidizing intolerant literature, low levels of literacy, high levels of poverty, and little taste for leisure reading (Schwartz et al., 2009). Our work suggests additional ones, also identified in the 2003 UNDP report. Rigid, centrally controlled education curricula whose content may not change for decades may not accommodate works for children with messages like these. However, a number of education reform efforts in the region suggest that the climate in education bureaucracies may be changing in a way that could increase receptivity for these materials. It would be worthwhile to better understand these reform efforts and the role that materials that support tolerance and critical thinking might play in new curricula and in library programs.

Despite the importance of parents in conveying attitudes, values, and support for literacy, we know little about their role in promoting media use, reading to their young children, and conveying messages about tolerance and support for critical thinking. Knowing more about parents' views concerning their responsibilities to their children in terms of literacy and societal values is key to understanding how tolerance might be spread more effectively. RAND's education reform work in the Gulf suggests that parents tend to view the schools as the experts in imparting key cultural values; they neither seek nor readily accept this role for themselves (Zellman et al., 2009).

To encourage the development and dissemination of materials that support these messages, it is critical to develop a range of thoughtful strategies. A fruitful place to start is to systematically examine gaps in our knowledge that, when filled, could help to more effectively direct efforts to improve the supply, distribution, and use of tolerance-supportive materials. The key gaps are noted below, along with ideas for addressing them.

Lack of good market data. A ready supply of attractive materials is necessary for successful promotion, distribution, and utilization of Arab-language materials that support children's development of tolerance and critical thinking. In our search for materials, we found many cheaply produced and unappealing books and other materials. We also encountered a number of publishers who expressed reluctance or outright unwillingness to invest in the development of high-quality materials for children. They noted a range of reasons for this reluctance, but most mentioned copyright issues. Some also mentioned the possibility of censorship, a barrier to the distribution of adult materials identified in earlier RAND work (Schwartz et al., 2009). A systematic survey of publishers, former publishers, and would-be publishers of children's materials, including those in more- and less-open countries, would enable us to examine perceptions about the market for children's tolerance-promoting materials, including private schools, ministries of education, libraries, and parents; explore their experiences with and concerns about censorship; better understand copyright issues and their effects on the works they publish and the production quality of those works; and elicit and discuss potential solutions to the problems identified.

Lack of clear understanding about piracy issues. In the course of collecting materials, we made a special effort to find cartoons and other television shows because they are likely to be seen by the most children. We heard repeatedly that the lack of such shows was a response to rampant piracy of these materials in the region. As long as would-be producers perceive that there is little if any potential for profits in developing cartoons and other television shows, they are unlikely to do so. We need to better understand the reality behind these perceptions, and what efforts, if any, are being directed to reducing piracy, what efforts might be required, and who might be engaged to make them.

It is important as well to look for targets of opportunity for getting these materials into the hands of children. We learned in our search that well-written, engaging materials, especially those for "tweens," are likely to find an audience once they are known. It would be worthwhile to analyze the opportunities provided by key cultural institutions, particularly schools and parents, to support the distribution of these materials.

A first effort would focus on examining the openness of schools and education ministries to including such materials in their curricula. A number of countries in the region have begun to make significant changes to their education systems, reforming or dismantling education ministries and their often rigid, highly prescriptive curricula. In a more open education space, these materials might find a place if they were better known, if teachers received training on how to employ them in social studies and other curricula, and if they were more accessible, e.g., through websites like Curriki, a website designed to create a community of educators, learners, and experts working together to develop and inform others of quality materials.[3]

Of equal importance, there could be considerable payoff from exploring the role that parents play in encouraging literacy and tolerance in their children. Research consistently identifies parents as the primary sources of influence on a host of outcomes for their children. Parents serve as the gatekeepers for the information and values that children are exposed to and that subsequently shape the values children adopt as their own. However, little is known about perceived parental roles or models of socialization in the Arab world. Such knowledge is critical in understanding the role that parents might play in promoting open-mindedness, tolerance, and critical thinking in their children. A survey of parents from different parts of the Arab world about their understanding of children and their own roles as parents, using surveys already fielded in the West, would help to clarify how parents view their roles and how they might be encouraged to support the socialization of tolerance.

It would also be worthwhile to consider ways to make the materials we found and screened widely accessible. One approach would be to make our catalog available on the Web. For example, it might be possible to work with a website like Curriki, where teachers go to find materials, to publicize the availability of our catalog. Another approach would be to work with libraries such as the renowned Bibliotheca Alexandrina in Egypt that makes many of its materials freely available through the Web. Similarly, it may be possible to build on local initiatives such as al-Hakawati (The Traditional Arab Storyteller) run by The Arab Cultural Trust, which already posts a number of tolerance-promoting children's stories on its website.

It might be advantageous as well to think about ways to reach out to Arabic-speaking children in the United States. In several parts of the country, e.g., the greater Detroit metropolitan area and areas of Northern Virginia, there are substantial populations of Arabic speakers. Including these materials in public library and school library collections could promote these values in Arabic-speaking communities in this country. In addition, placing these materials in public places reinforces the value of openness and tolerance on which this country is based.

It would also be worthwhile, given low levels of literacy and little leisure reading, to find ways to convert or adapt printed works with constructive themes for other media, particularly television. Portraying appealing stories and characters through television programs represents a promising vehicle for reaching Arab children, given the high penetration of satellite television programming in the region.

Finally, some direct testing of the appropriateness of the materials and their short-term impact on children's attitudes would be beneficial. Specifically, simple pre- and post-tests of levels of tolerance or critical thinking before and after exposure to some of the materials we identified would provide valuable information about their effectiveness and the utility of the concepts that we used in identifying and selecting them.

All these efforts could be employed by local policymakers and educators to support the development of tolerance and critical thinking in young children in the Arab world. Such

---

[3] See www.curriki.org.

efforts could help to build a knowledge society characterized by openness and critical thinking, dispositions that lead their holders to be motivated to learn from other cultures and to support new, more-open ideas.

Research on the Teaching of Tolerance and Critical Thinking

In contrast to the literature on the acquisition of tolerance and critical thinking, the literature on the teaching of these dispositions focuses more heavily on critical thinking. This no doubt reflects the greater involvement of cognitive mechanisms in critical thinking and the alignment of these skills with broader education goals in many countries. In contrast, teaching of tolerance may engage political issues that schools and teachers may prefer to ignore.

The literature on preschoolers suggests that they, like school-aged children, can be taught interpersonal skills, critical thinking skills, and some ability to consider the perspectives of others in the classroom. Aboud and Levy (2000) describe five broad types of interventions that aim to reduce prejudice; most occur in school settings. They include ethnically integrated schooling and bilingual education, which increase intergroup contact; multicultural and anti-racist education, which socializes children to and reinforces group norms of tolerance; training in social and cognitive skills associated with the development of critical thinking; and role-playing and training in empathy, which are designed to address emotional reactions to out-groups. All have been found to be effective to some degree. Aboud and Fenwick (1999) found, for example, that an 11-week classroom-based intervention during which teachers discussed the value of processing internal attributes rather than people's race reduced prejudice in black and white 5th graders. Another study (Aboud and Doyle, 1996) found that when prejudiced 3rd and 4th graders were paired with less-prejudiced friends to discuss how the races should be evaluated, the prejudiced students became less prejudiced. They concluded that talking about race and racial attitudes in school settings can reduce prejudice. Hanley et al. (2007) found that instructions, modeling, role-play, and feedback helped preschoolers develop and demonstrate pro-social skills such as following instructions, functional communication, ability to tolerate delay, and friendship skills. At least some of these (e.g., explicit instruction and positive role models) can be provided through less-dynamic media, such as books, television, and Internet. These skills were taught during circle time, free play, transitions, and meals. The evaluation of this effort revealed that the program resulted in a 74-percent reduction in problem behavior and a more than fourfold increase in preschool life skills (Hanley et al., 2007).

Data from studies of elementary school students have shown that active teacher behaviors designed to promote critical thinking and thinking strategies appear to be effective in building these skills. Trepanier and Romatowski (1982) described an intervention for 1st graders that consisted of reading selected children's books that focused on sharing or on an interpersonal conflict that was successfully resolved through sharing during regularly scheduled story-telling times. The reading time included teacher use of planned critical thinking questions that focused on interpersonal conflict, the feelings of each character, the cause of their feelings, and the resolution of the conflict by sharing. Pre- and post-testing revealed that students who were exposed to the reading and questions were more likely to suggest sharing as a solution to interpersonal conflicts than students who were not exposed to the intervention. Corral-Verdugo, Frias-Armenta, and Corral-Verdugo (1996) found that teaching strategies helped to promote 8–10-year-old Mexican students' abilities to distinguish between environmental facts and opinions. These strategies included giving examples, providing feedback, and reinforcing the distinction between fact and opinion. Block (1993) found that students in grades 2–6 who were given a lesson that focused on thinking and reading comprehension strategies and who then applied those strategies as they read children's literature scored significantly higher on standardized tests of reading comprehension, on the ability to transfer cognitive strategies to situations outside of school, and on measures of self-esteem and critical and creative thinking.

Perkins and Ritchhart (2004) note that a useful approach to promoting thinking that they have found in their work with students in grades 4–8 in the United States and Sweden is for teachers to develop thinking routines in the classroom. These routines, like other classroom routines, become part of the way that students do things in the classroom. These routines operate at the sociocultural level because they are acquired in group settings, but they are gradually internalized as individual thinking habits. The routines generally involve simple procedures or practices that are used frequently. One example of a thinking routine is brainstorming, which is designed to promote openness and flexibility. It is a generic skill with wide applicability across subjects and grade levels. Another routine noted by Perkins and Ritchhart is the "take a stance" routine, in which students defend a position. Knowing that such activities are expected increases students' inclination to think carefully as they read and think. Television shows that model brainstorming and may even pose direct questions to children, providing them with an opportunity to pause and reflect, may mimic some of this effect.

Several studies suggest processes that promote critical thinking and tolerance in elementary school students. A Turkish study found that teaching history through stories that included people of different religions and ethnicities influenced students' ideas about people from different cultural backgrounds in a positive way. Further, the stories helped students appreciate the importance of tolerance (Demircioglu, 2008). Another study (Edwards and Foss, 2000) used two picture books on the internment of Japanese Americans by the U.S. government during World War II to help 8th graders learn how truth is often found through examining multiple perspectives. Sadler (1993) presents a strategy for teaching critical thinking skills to elementary and middle school students through the use of logic problems. Through the construction and modification of these problems, students learn to think about problems in multiple ways, a process that is believed to promote critical thinking. Sadler offers a "semantic map," as well as worksheets, charts, and blank statements needed to solve these problems. Riesenmy et al. (1991) relied on small-group discussions in ten 4th and 5th grade classrooms to help students develop four thinking roles: task definer, strategist, monitor, and challenger. Compared with similar students who did not receive this training, the students in the experiment used more information to reach solutions, had higher levels of self-directed thinking skills, and produced higher-quality answers in a post-test.

A study of high-school-aged students (McAlister et al., 2000) found that at this age, peer modeling of tolerance in student newsletters promoted intergroup tolerance and moral engagement, decreased verbal aggression, and produced fewer hostile behavioral intentions.

It is generally understood that the influence of schools and classrooms may go well beyond what teachers teach: They can also function as an important social context—for the youngest children, often one of the few contexts beyond the family to which they are exposed. As such, teachers may play a key role in socializing ideas about tolerance (and, of course, intolerance). The social context of the classroom is largely established by the teacher, who can create an atmosphere that encourages critical thinking and tolerance (Perkins and Ritchhart, 2004). Teachers can reinforce positive social behaviors and promote tolerance on a daily basis. Principals and other school leaders can create an environment that supports tolerance and encourages or discourages opportunities for children to learn about and get to know children who differ from them.

Perkins and Ritchhart (2004) distinguish between instilling critical thinking skills through creating a classroom culture that supports such thinking and teaching thinking skills more directly. They describe the former as creating a classroom climate in which thinking is "welcome" (p. 375) and reinforced, and promoting such thinking through focusing on big ideas, including opportunities for student choice and self-direction, encouraging students' intellectual independence or autonomy, and providing time for thinking. Teachers help to create a climate of support for thinking by conveying the value they place on it, stressing the importance of curiosity, inquiry, and playing with ideas. By recognizing students' thoughtful contributions and demonstrating genuine interest in students' ideas, teachers make clear that thinking and associated questioning are valued. Teachers can also build a climate of support by helping students experience what they call *cognitive emotions*: joy at verification, surprise at unexpected outcomes, and the thrill of discovery. These emotions, they contend, convey to students that thinking has intrinsic rewards and benefits. But as Perkins and Ritchhart (2004) note, welcoming and supporting student thinking is not enough. Students still need to know how to think.

Conclusions

The education literature clearly focuses on the teacher as a key factor in setting the classroom social environment and in teaching and reinforcing the use of critical thinking skills. As noted in the body of this report, these classroom-focused strategies had little direct relevance to the criteria we developed or the materials we selected and reviewed, because they are so teacher-dependent. Our assumption, discussed above, was that in most cases children would be alone when relating to the materials we selected. Nevertheless, as discussed previously, it may be possible to inject the guidance and support that a teacher or other adult might bring into some materials through interactive content, either in the form of TV shows that ask participants questions or in which adults or slightly older peers model desired behaviors, or in the course of video games or other web-based materials.

Table of Relevant Skills by Age

In Table B.1, we summarize—for each of the attributes that children acquire over time relevant to the development of tolerance and critical thinking—the key skills they generally acquire during each of the three age groupings included in our study. These skills, along with the key theoretical concepts discussed above, guided the development of the coding categories discussed in Chapter Three.

Table B.1
Developmental Stages and Corresponding Abilities

Age Group	Cognitive Development[1]	Ability to Take the Perspective of Others[2]	Moral Development[3]	Emotion and Emotion Understanding
Early years (ages 4–6) Preoperational stage	Children become increasingly aware that make-believe and other thoughts are not real (e.g., young children believe that Clark Kent truly does become superman). Across this period, children replace magical beliefs/ events that violate expectations with more-plausible explanations. Children are able to grasp only a single storyline at a time.	Children's ability to infer what others are feeling and thinking is limited. Children recognize that the self and others can have different thoughts and feelings, but they frequently confuse the two.	Early in this stage, fear of authority and avoidance of punishment are reasons for behaving morally. Later, satisfying personal needs determines moral choice. Children at this stage display differentiated understanding of the legitimacy of authority figures. They can distinguish between moral rules, social conventions, and matters of personal choice. Children at this stage base distributive justice on equality (fairness involves equal distribution of goods regardless of need).	Vivid imaginations combined with difficulty separating appearance from reality make fears common in early childhood. Adults may want to limit exposure to frightening stories during this period. Understanding of causes, consequences, and behavioral signs of emotion improves in accuracy and complexity. Discussions about others' feelings and how different feelings lead to people's behaviors help children develop emotional understanding. Media that expose children to such discussions, especially to people whose views differ, should be helpful to children.

Table B.1—Continued

Age Group	Cognitive Development[1]	Ability to Take the Perspective of Others[2]	Moral Development[3]	Emotion and Emotion Understanding
Middle years (ages 7–10) Concrete operational stage	Thinking becomes more logical, flexible, and organized about concrete information. Children are now good at thinking about concrete things. Around ages 9–11 children are able to integrate multiple plot dimensions and can tell coherent stories with a main plot and several subplots.	Children understand that different perspectives may result from people having access to different information (ages 4–9, according to Selman). Children can step into another person's shoes and view thoughts, feelings and behavior from the other person's perspective. They also recognize that others can do the same. Children begin to understand that people's prior knowledge and beliefs influence how they understand the events unfolding around them.	Early in this stage, maintaining the affection and approval of friends and relatives motivates good behavior. Later, a duty to uphold laws and rules for their own sake justifies moral conformity. At this stage, children are able to take more factors into account in distinguishing moral rules, social conventions, and matters of personal choice. For example, the concept of fairness depends on the specifics of a situation (e.g., need or effort are taken into account in making decisions about dividing resources).	Rapid gains in emotional self-regulation (the ability to control one's emotions) occur after school entry. Children become better at understanding conflicting cues in explaining others' emotions. The understanding that people can experience multiple emotions at one time is solidified. Children's understanding that people's expression of feelings (e.g., their facial expressions) may not reflect people's true feelings increases.
Adolescence (11–adulthood) Formal operational stage *Because of a lack of opportunity to solve hypothetical problems, formal operational reasoning is not evident in all societies.*	Abstract, scientific reasoning emerges. Children do not need a concrete referent to evaluate the logic of a statement. Children begin to understand premises that contradict reality. Adolescents can come up with new, more-general logic rules through internal thought and reflection. Kids believe that they are the focus of everyone else's attention (lessens after age 14). Most believe that they are special and unique (after age 14 this begins to subside).	Children can step outside a two-person situation and imagine how the self and other are viewed from the perspective of a third, impartial party.	Fair procedures for changing laws to protect individual rights and the needs of the majority are emphasized. Abstract universal principles that are valid for all humanity guide moral decisionmaking.	Late in adolescence children develop more complex empathy as they begin to understand that others lead continuous lives beyond their current situations (e.g., the ability to empathize with the poor or oppressed who have had to deal with ongoing adverse circumstances).

[1] Based on Piaget's breakdown of developmental stage and follow-up research to Piaget's work.
[2] Based on the stages in Selman (1971).
[3] Based on Kohlberg (1976). The text after the gap in each entry augments Kohlberg.

Coding Manual and Coding Form

Material and Author Description (Page One)

Please fill in the first set of boxes before coding the actual material (which begins with age level targeted on page 2). Include your name, check type of work, note its title with English translation, transliteration and in Arabic (and other languages, if appropriate). Briefly describe the author's background, which if possible, should include country of origin, current location, gender, educational background, profession, cultural and political background, e.g., member of a religious minority? And whether the author consistently produces tolerant and/or critical thinking material or if the coded material is unusual for this author. Also note publication information: language in which work is available, first edition data, ISBN number (if available), and number of pages.

In your coding, please pay careful attention to any pictures, as they may convey important but subtle messages that we want to be sure to include in our assessment of the work.

A. Age Level Targeted

Note whether the material appears to be targeted to children in their early years (4-6), middle years (7–10) or adolescents (11–14). Font size and length of sentences may provide clues about the age group targeted. Note that for the youngest group, we don't necessarily expect that they will be able to read the material themselves; this should not be a criterion in selecting age level targeted. The key is that the concepts and visuals are appropriate for the youngest group. See *Developmental Stages and Corresponding Abilities* table for help as needed to code age level.

B. One Gender Targeted?

Check whether the work is targeted to males or females. If there is no apparent targeting, check both the male and female boxes.

C. Content

1. Diversity among Characters

Diversity. The aim of this code is to capture whether the material portrays diverse or non-homogeneous characters, deals with diversity in more subtle ways, or makes a broader argument about the value of diversity. We are very interested in capturing diversity and expect that most of it will be captured in the first category, *Character diversity*. The other diversity categories were largely created to make sure that we did not exclude materials that we thought were valuable, such as *I Live*, which portrays a single, non-diverse family. If you find and code for character diversity, you will in all likelihood not need to code for any other type of diversity.

a. Character diversity may be found in ethnic background, religion, native country, social class, level of religiosity, or abilities (e.g., a blind child among sighted children). In nonhuman characters, character diversity may manifest itself in terms of size, color, species, etc., e.g., cats and dogs, or butterflies of different colors. If there is just one character or one homogeneous family portrayed in the material, use this code *only* if the single character or family is a member of a minority **independent of context**, e.g., blind or handicapped. If the diversity is more contextually dependent, e.g., a divorced family that is not portrayed as diverse in any other way is presented as cooperating in co-parenting their child in a way that is not typical in the Middle East, **do not use this code**. Instead, consider using the *Arab World Diversity* code below.

Exclusion Criteria: Don't code for character diversity if the material portrays Western or Arab children who are not diverse, or if there is a single Western or Arab child portrayed.

b. Self-perceived diversity may be found in materials in which the characters may be quite similar demographically (e.g., same nation, same ethnic group, same religion) but see themselves as different or are portrayed as different. The difference may be based on another less obvious characteristic (e.g., tribe, socio-economic status), or the difference may become apparent as the story unfolds, e.g., one child who is quite artistic doesn't fit in with the other children, all of whom are quite athletic and like to play soccer; the lead character who is undergoing a lot of scrutiny and judgment is wearing rougher clothes and looks like he is poorer than the other characters. Check this category even if there is no major difference between characters or groups but it is obvious that one or more characters perceive themselves as different from those in another group; there are distinctions made between "us" and "them" in the material.

c. Allegorical diversity refers to diversity that is portrayed or discussed through allegory or metaphor rather than characters. A good example may be found in the book, *Pink, Pink, Pink*, where a girl and her parents are not diverse, but the story talks about how she likes to wear, eat, and relate only to pink things. She learns over the course of the story that just one color is boring and embraces other colors. Other allegorical diversity might also be found if a story's characters, all of whom are members of the same family and therefore not diverse, are looking at a rainbow and admiring the many colors.

d. Arab World diversity refers to diversity that is *not* part of the material itself and only becomes evident when the character or characters portrayed in the material or their behaviors and ways of thinking are compared against the characteristics of the Arab world as a whole. For example, *I Live* (Ana Askoun) portrays a divorced family in which the parents live separately, but are portrayed as working closely together to parent their son and convey to him that he is loved and that the divorce is not his fault. While divorce is increasingly common in the Arab world, the sort of involved, cooperative co-parenting described in this book's text and illustrations is not. So while *I Live* portrays a single family and no diversity is presented or implied (for example, you might code for character diversity if the mother is portrayed as Palestinian and the father Syrian), the way they handle co-parenting is quite different than is typical in the Arab world.

This is a challenging code because of course the Arab world is itself diverse, and therefore this code should be considered *only* when the other diversity codes don't apply. Since each of the coders comes from a different country and has had very different experiences in and with the Arab world, if you are uncertain about whether this code applies, please query the Arabickids@rand.org alias for discussion and guidance.

For the next sets of codes, Relationships, Actions, Thinking, and Emotion, the same material content may be used to code more than one category. For example, in *Three Butterflies*, the sun stops the rain because the butterflies refuse to desert each other when the flowers offer to protect only the butterfly of the same color as they are. This action on the part of the sun and the statement the sun makes might be used to code Supportive consequences of relationships *and* Supportive consequences of actions, *and* Supportive commentary on relationships *and* actions. It also might be used for codes in the Thinking and Emotions categories.

2. Relationships among Characters

The aim of these codes is to capture whether the nature of the characters' relationships conveys a message of tolerance and acceptance. This can be done in several ways: by showing characters relating positively to each other, by showing characters relating negatively to each other, by including some commentary on their relationship that reflects positively on a positive relationship and negatively on a negative one, and by showing positive consequences from getting along or negative consequences from not getting along. There are three main categories: relationships among characters, supportive commentary on relationships, and supportive consequences of relationships. In using these categories, we make a distinction between central or instrumental characters and other characters. Central characters are vital to the story; the story would not be able to proceed as written without them. It may help to think about this concept as "instrumental characters," because it is not about how frequently a character appears, but his or her role in the story that matters. For example, in *Three Butterflies*, the sun makes only a brief appearance at the end of the story, but is a central character because he chooses to reward the butterflies' commitment to each other by stopping the rain. In contrast, in *I Live*, the parents set up the context of the story but are not part of the story directly. So the parents would not be considered central characters.

How characters relate codes for how characters are shown relating to each other. Check whichever of the three codes is closest. For each of these codes, feel free to code "close to yes" if there are elements of the code present but the presentation is subtle or you are a bit uncertain. "Close to yes" and "yes" codes are treated the same, so don't spend a lot of time trying to decide which to use.

a. The characters get along throughout the work. Check this box if none of the central/instrumental characters fight with each other or disagree at any time. *Close to yes:* Check this box if the central characters have one or more minor disagreements but remain emotionally and/or physically close throughout the work. Also check this box if other, non-instrumental characters have significant disagreements but they do not affect the central characters. In coding here, it is important to understand who is considered a central or instrumental character, as noted above. Instrumental characters are defined as characters who are central to the story: Without that character, the story would not be able to proceed as written. So, in *Three Butterflies,* the butterflies, the flowers, and the sun are all central characters and so their relationships and feelings should be coded. In *I Live*, the parents set up the context of the story but are not part of the story directly. So the parents would not be considered central characters.

Exclusion criteria: There is significant fighting or disagreement among at least two of the central characters.

b. The central characters resolve differences and get along at the end. Check this box if the central characters don't get along at the beginning but resolve their differences at some point in the story and are getting along at the end. *Close to yes*: Check this box if the instrumental characters resolve differences at the end but are not emotionally or physically close at the end. Also check this box if other characters resolve differences and get along at the end.

Exclusion criteria: There are no differences among the characters; any differences are not resolved at the end.

c. The central characters don't get along throughout. Check this box if the central/instrumental characters don't get along at the beginning and never resolve these differences, so they are emotionally distant throughout. *Close to yes*: Check this box if other characters don't get along throughout.

Exclusion criteria: Don't check this box if characters don't ever disagree or resolve their differences in the course of the work.

d. Supportive consequences of relationships. Check this box if *actual consequences* result from the characters' relationship. The presentation of the consequences may be part of the story itself, reported by another character, or noted by a narrator or in additional materials attached to the work, e.g., a discussion section at the end of a chapter. The consequences should be positive when there is a positive relationship described in the material, and negative when there is a negative relationship. For example, if two characters do not get along, to check this box we should see negative consequences in the story that result from their not getting along (e.g., they argue about who will get the balloon, and while they are arguing, a dog comes along and pops it). Alternatively, another character can tell us that neither child got to play with the balloon because while they fought over it, a dog grabbed it and popped it. In *Three Butterflies*, we see a supportive consequence of relationships clearly: The sun steps in to stop the rain in response to the butterflies' determination to stick together and not accept the flowers' offer to shelter only the butterfly that is the same color.

Exclusion criteria: Don't check this box if there are no consequences from good or bad relationships presented in the work or its appended materials. Don't check this box if bad outcomes are presented as possibilities rather than as something that actually happened. If this sort of material is present, check the category below.

e. Supportive commentary on relationships. Check this box if one or more of the central characters, a narrator, or another character in the work makes *explicit* comments about the characters' relationships. The commentary should be positive when there is a positive relationship described in the material, and negative when there is a negative relationship. If two kids are fighting over a toy in the story, a commentary might note how when kids fight about toys, neither of them enjoy them because the child who loses feels the loss, and the child who "wins" may feel bad for making his peer cry or feel sad. If the characters start out not getting along but later resolve their differences, the commentary may note how much better things went once they started to get along with each other. In *Three Butterflies,* the sun expresses happiness because the three butterflies decide not to separate by color to seek shelter from the rain. This category is important for young children because they may not be able to draw these conclusions themselves, and we don't know if a parent or other adult will be there to do it for them. We probably don't want to see a lot of these explicit commentaries in materials for older children; they will interpret it as preachiness and might therefore reject the message.

It is likely that if you check this box, you will also check the box on *Supportive commentary on actions*, although you do not have to check both, if, for example, you see a positive relationship on which comments are made but no actions.

Exclusion criteria: Don't check this box if there is no discussion about the good things about good relationships, e.g., they make you feel good, or the disadvantages of bad relationships, e.g., they make you feel bad or socially isolated.

3. Actions

The aim of this set of codes is to capture the actions of the characters. The actions highlighted are those that model tolerance, pro-social behaviors such as kindness, sharing, comforting of others, altruism (putting the needs of others before one's own), and other friendly overtures. If it is a stranger, a friendly overture may legitimately be limited to saying "hello."

a. At least one character acts in a tolerant or pro-social way. Check this box if at least one character acts in a tolerant or pro-social way (it is not necessary that all do). *Pro-social* refers to behaviors such as kindness, sharing, comforting of others, altruism, and other friendly overtures. If the material does not include diverse groups e.g., it is the story of one family (who is different from other, non-portrayed families), you may still use this code if there is tolerance or kindness portrayed in the story to the characters in it.

Exclusion criteria: If a child becomes intolerant over the course of the story and is not reprimanded or does not suffer negative consequences for this, do not check this category for tolerance.

b. Supportive consequences from tolerant or pro-social actions. Check this box if there are *actual positive consequences* that derive from the tolerant or pro-social actions, and/or negative consequences that derive from intolerant or anti-social actions.

Exclusion criteria: One unlikely scenario is that a child behaving in a tolerant way is reprimanded for doing so. If this happens, do not check this box because tolerance has led to negative consequences. However, if the criticizer is himself criticized so that the child is ultimately rewarded for his tolerance, do check this box.

c. Supportive commentary on tolerant or pro-social actions. Check this box if there is discussion about how good it is that the tolerant character is behaving well or that it is not good that the intolerant character is behaving badly. This commentary may come from any character, a narrator, or appended materials.

Exclusion criteria: Do not check this box if there are no tolerant or pro-social actions or if there is no commentary about them in the material.

4. Thinking

The aim of this set of codes is to identify materials that support openmindedness by portraying diverse ways of thinking. The following three codes are available. For each of these codes we want to capture whether the message is strengthened through supportive commentary about the behavior.

a. Different ways to think or solve a problem are discussed or shown. Check this box if the material portrays individual characters or groups taking the same elements of a situation and putting them together in different ways to solve a problem or understand what is happening. For example, if two characters are asked what is the best way to deal with a situation where they see a child being bullied on the schoolyard, one character could respond with "tell the teacher" while another could respond with "go and support the child being bullied." Both are reasonable ways to respond; this indicates that there may be more than one way to respond to or solve a problem. If there is this sort of discussion or lesson in the material, check the box. Note that anyone can present this idea that there are multiple ways to address problems: It may occur through a narrator or one or more characters, central or not; different ways to think or solve a problem may be shown through narration, what happens in the story, or through the thoughts of any of the characters. Note as well that characters may come up with different solutions because their motivations are different; this is fine. The key is that for whatever reason, the material presents different ways to solve a problem. For example, in *And on That Night*, the shaikhs cover up the key water source to reduce inter-tribal conflict; the sons of the two shaikhs, who are close friends, uncover the water source so that the tribes do not leave the area, which would mean the friends would be separated.

Exclusion criteria: Do not check this box if the material does not demonstrate in some way that characters responded to the situation in different ways, all of which have some validity. Do not check this box if different approaches are shown but one approach is presented as the "right" one and another approach is presented as "wrong." For example, if one child on a treasure hunt uses clues in a particular way and wins, and the other gets lost and doesn't claim the prize, then do not check this box.

b. Supportive commentary on different ways to think or solve a problem. Check this box if the material makes positive statements about the fact that the characters thought about things in different ways, e.g., "there is more than one good way to think about a problem or situation." This support may be found in narration, through the words or actions of any of the characters, and through appended materials. Also check the box if the material notes that *not* thinking creatively, or *not* coming up with different ways to solve a problem, meant that the problem wasn't solved, or wasn't solved as well as it could have been.

Exclusion criteria: Do not check this box if there is no problem-solving going on, or if there is no discussion of the problem-solving process and its outcomes.

c. Question rules, authority or societal assumptions while thinking or problem solving. This code captures whether characters question rules, authority, or societal assumptions as they solve problems, try to understand a situation, or try to meet their own goals or others' needs. As was noted in our staff discussions, terrorists question authority too. We are certainly not looking for those kind of messages, in which the replacement of one ideology or set of rules with another is advocated. What we are looking for here is not rebellion against authority but thinking for one's self in a respectful way. Check this box if a narrator, any character, or any appended materials convey this respectful questioning process. For example, check this box if a child is told she cannot do something because she is a girl and she thinks that this doesn't make sense and goes to discuss this rule with her mother.

Exclusion criteria: Do not check this box if no rules or authorities are questioned in the problem-solving process or if no problem-solving is going on. Do not check this box if the questioning is disrespectful or if the questioning involves replacing one set of rules with another. Do not check this box if it is not clear what the societal assumptions are; don't think too much about this! In *Three Butterflies*, the butterflies question the apparent rule that the flowers apply, which is that butterfly colors should match flower colors. The group concluded that this is *not* an example of societal assumptions operating, because the societal assumptions are not explicitly discussed in the story.

d. Supportive commentary for questioning rules, authority or societal assumptions while problem-solving. Check this box if there is commentary that supports the questioning of rules, authority, or societal assumptions. It might involve discussing how there were negative outcomes in the story for failing to question and/or positive outcomes for doing so. There might be discussion about how it is sometimes hard to do this, but that it is important. This commentary could come from a narrator, any character, or appended materials.

Exclusion criteria: Do not check this box if there is no discussion about the value of questioning authority, rules, or assumptions.

e. Draw different conclusions from the same information. Check this box if the material shows that people have different perspectives and reasonably can draw different conclusions from the same information. For example, if the weather is rainy one child might decide to stay indoors while another might decide that it would be fun to go outside and play in the puddles. Both are legitimate perspectives and this point is made in the material.

Exclusion criteria: Do not check this box if the characters do not draw different conclusions from the same information.

f. Supportive commentary for acknowledging different perspectives. Check this box if there is discussion about how there are positive outcomes for acknowledging and embracing different perspectives and conclusions, and/or negative outcomes for not doing so. This commentary may come from any of the characters, from the narrator, or from appended materials.

Exclusion criteria: Do not check this box if different perspectives are not presented in the material, or if there is no discussion or consequences of the benefits of allowing or embracing different conclusions from the same information.

5. Emotions

The aim of this set of codes is to identify materials in which open-mindedness is conveyed through presentation of the complexity of feelings. This complexity can be expressed either through complex feelings in one person or by showing different reactions that multiple people have to the same situation. These feelings can include both positive and negative feelings. For example, if a story portrays one child hitting another in the schoolyard, a single child who observes the hitting might have complex feelings, e.g., anger at the child who was aggressive, empathy for the child who was hit. Or that child might have even more complex feelings, e.g., both anger at the aggressor and empathy for him, if the aggressor was hit by the victim last week. Or, the work might portray multiple children who witness the aggression. One feels angry at the aggressor, while another feels empathy for the victim but fear about coming to the victim's aid or standing up to the aggressor.

This category of emotions is important because if people can accept the complexity of their own feelings they will find it easier to accept that others may not always have the same feelings as they do in reaction to a given situation. This understanding that people can reasonably have different emotional reactions to the same situation contributes to the promotion of tolerance.

Note that the goal of this section is to identify materials where emotional complexity is supported. The emotional complexity may involve emotions that might not seem appropriate, e.g., being happy when a child's school burns down. It is not about making decisions that are good or appropriate.

a. Some age-appropriate emotional complexity is presented. Check this box if some emotional complexity is conveyed, for example, more than one emotion is conveyed. Check this box if one character experiences more than one emotion at the same time, or if multiple characters experience different emotions in reaction to the same situation, e.g., if a child is teased, one child may think it is funny while another child is upset by the teasing. Or, the same child may first enjoy watching a child get teased, then feel bad later for not supporting the child who was being teased. *Close to yes*: Check this box if you believe you are seeing multiple emotions portrayed but their portrayal seems quite subtle, or if one emotion is very clearly displayed and other emotions are less obvious but you believe they are there. For this code, feel free to check "close to yes" if there are elements of the code present but the presentation is subtle or you are a bit uncertain.

Exclusion criteria: Do not check this box if emotions are not presented in the material, either verbally, e.g., a child says, "I am really happy that the school burned down so we don't have to go" or nonverbally, e.g., a child cries when she sees the burned-out school, or through narration. Do not check this box if *all* the emotions are very subtle and you find yourself not sure if you are seeing them or not.

b. Supportive consequences of considering emotional complexity. Check this box if the work presents negative outcomes for failing to consider that people may have complex emotional reactions to situations, or that different people may react with different emotions to the same event. Also check this box if the work describes or presents positive consequences for considering one or both of these things. These consequences may be part of the story, or be presented by the characters or a narrator.

Exclusion criteria: Do not check this box if multiple emotions are not displayed or if there are no consequences presented.

c. Supportive commentary on emotions expressed. Check this box if there is commentary about the fact that people can have different emotional responses to the same situation. For example, there may be discussion of the fact that different people can have different reactions to the same situation, or that one person may have conflicting emotions in response to the same situation, either at the same time or at different times. This commentary may be provided by any of the characters, by the narrator, or by addendum material.

Exclusion criteria: Do not check this box if emotions are not presented in the material, or they are presented but in a way that is not noted explicitly.

6. Presentational Elements That Facilitate Learning of the Material's Content or Lessons

a. Opportunities for Active Learning

The next set of codes identifies characteristics of the content that increase the likelihood that children will internalize/benefit from the positive messages that are conveyed in the material. This category is intended to capture the extent to which the potential user is drawn into the material and encouraged to make some response. This is important because the literature finds that active learning helps children focus and better absorb the material.

We have determined that opportunities for active learning may sometimes be subtle but should still be coded. For example, in "I'm the Best Child in the World," the story ends with the main character sitting alone while the other children play and swim together. The question is posed, "...Why did none of them want to play with [Hani] the main character? Didn't his mother tell him that everyone would like him?" While these questions may reflect Hani's internal thoughts, the fact that there are questions posed may well engage the reader, and encourage the reader to think about these issues as well. For this reason, Opportunities for Active Learning should be coded here.

For each category, enter a zero if you see "none", a 1 if you see "some", and a 2 if you see a lot of the element. This is a subjective judgment based on the material as a whole, so rely on your judgment.

1. *Active learning opportunities.* This box assesses if, for example, the work presents situations where information is provided but the child/user is asked to draw his/her own conclusions, or to contextualize the content in their own experience. For example, the child may have an opportunity to respond or test their assumptions before additional information is provided. This condition may be most often found in computer games, although some books facilitate active reader involvement as well, often by posing questions, which may make the child pause to think of possible answers or solutions. Another example of active learning may be found in books that have activities mapped out in the text to extend children's learning from and enjoyment of the material. Use your judgment about whether you are seeing "none," "some," or "a lot."

2. *Interactivity* captures the extent to which exchanges are built into the content. Enter a 1 or 2 even if there is merely a "pretense" of interactivity. For example, if a character on a television show turns to the viewers and asks for their opinion/help/involvement, check this code even if, in fact, a child's response or lack thereof has no bearing on what happens next. For example, in the show "Dora the Explorer," young viewers are asked to say "Swiper No Swiping!" when a fox named Swiper tried to steal from the central character. In "Little Einsteins," another TV show, children are asked to clap to power the characters' spacecraft. Use your judgment about whether you are seeing "none," "some," or "a lot."

3. *Scaffolding* refers to situations where the message is simplified for the viewer in one of the following two ways:

1. The work breaks down more-complex content to make the message easier to understand. For example, in a story where child A hurt child B's feelings, an adult may explain to child A how child B is feeling, they may point to child B's face and say: "look, he's feeling very sad. Do you know why he's sad?" etc.

2. The work draws explicit conclusions to make sure children get the "right" message from the content. For example, following from the example above, the adult might note that child A's actions caused child B to feel bad and explicitly tell child A to apologize, attempt to reconcile, or compensate child B as appropriate.

Put a 1 or 2 in the scaffolding box if you see any evidence of this going on in the material you are rating. Enter a zero if you see none. Use your judgment about whether you are seeing "none," "some," or "a lot."

If you have checked "Supportive Commentary" earlier, you probably will check scaffolding, as they are quite similar. Scaffolding can refer to any part of the story, while supportive commentary codes are linked to particular aspects.

b. Other Positive Presentational Elements

1. *Engaging visuals or other aspects of presentation.* Put a 1 or 2 in this box when there is engaging art or other non-message aspects of the presentation. Use your judgment about whether you are seeing "some" or "a lot." If the visuals are unappealing or just ordinary, enter a zero.

2. *Engaging story, plot, or structure.* Put a 1 or 2 in this box if the content of the material is interesting, has appealing/engaging characters, etc. Use your judgment about whether you

are seeing "some" or "a lot." If these aspects of the material are boring, stilted, or confusing, enter a zero.

3. *Engaging language.* Enter a 1 or 2 in this box if the material is appealing because the text is well-written, uses colorful metaphors, etc. Check this box as well if there is use of invented words, rhymes, interesting names, or other words that make the text appealing to children in the targeted age range. Use your judgment about whether you are seeing "some" or "a lot." If the language is boring, stilted, or confusing, enter a zero.

c. Cultural Insensitivity

To the extent possible, we are eliminating materials that risk being culturally offensive or insensitive from our catalog of materials to be coded. However, if you do find that some element of the material creates a risk that the material may be perceived as insensitive, please check this box. If you are uncertain, if there are elements of the code present but the presentation is subtle or you are a bit uncertain, feel free to check "1". If there are no problems, enter "0"; serious problems should receive a "2" code.

This is a tough one, because we don't want to be too timid by excluding materials that take any risks at all. At the same time, we don't want some perceived insensitivity to overshadow the positive messages in a work. This category is located under presentational elements because we think that much depends on presentation. For example, in the film *Captain Abu Raed,* a boy is removed from his abusive father, which is generally unacceptable in these cultures. But it is done after portraying serious abuse and is done in a sensitive way. That movie also portrays a young single woman offering a ride in her car to an older man, Captain Abu Raed. We also talked about a story in which there is a picture of a girl wearing a short skirt; concerns were raised about whether this would distract from the positive story messages. A clear example of something that undermines a work is a story we discussed in which Jordanian and Palestinian children bond in antipathy toward Israelis.

Enter a 1 or 2 in this box if the material portrays, in text, pictures, commentary, or activities, messages that may undermine the acceptability of the work and its messages. If the work has no element of insensitivity, enter a 0.

CODING FORM

REVIEWER of this work: [   ]

Type of Work:

☐ Novel ☐ Movie ☐ Play ☐ Non-fiction ☐ Video Game ☐ Cartoon
☐ Magazine ☐ Short-story/ies ☐ Other (Please Specify:_____)

Title of Work - English Translation: [   ]

Title of Work - Transliteration: [   ]

Title of Work - in Arabic: [   ]

Title of Work - in Other Languages: [   ]

Author's name - in Arabic: [   ]

Author's name - Transliteration: [   ]

Author's background (if possible, note country of origin, gender, education background, profession, cultural and political background [e.g., religious minority?]):

[   ]

Work is Available in: ☐ Arabic ☐ English ☐ French ☐ Other, Specify:
[   ]

Publication Information: [   ]

Date of First Edition: [   ]

ISBN Number: [   ]

Number of Pages: [   ]

A. AGE LEVEL TARGETED

Early years (4–6) ☐

Middle years (7–10) ☐

Adolescence (11–14) ☐

B. ONE GENDER TARGETED? (Check one or both)

Male ☐

Female ☐

C. CONTENT

1. Diversity among Characters

a. Character Diversity ☐

b. Self-perceived Diversity ☐

c. Allegorical Diversity ☐

d. Arab World Diversity ☐

2. Relationships among Characters

How characters relate

a. Get along throughout ☐

   1. Close to yes ☐

b. Resolve differences and get along at the end ☐

   1. Close to yes ☐

c. Don't get along throughout ☐

   1. Close to yes ☐

d. Supportive consequences on relationships ☐

e. Supportive commentary of relationships ☐

3. Actions

a. At least one character acts in a tolerant or pro-social way ☐

b. Supportive consequences from tolerant or pro-social actions ☐

c. Supportive commentary on tolerant or pro-social actions ☐

4. Thinking

a. Different ways to think or solve a problem are discussed or shown ☐

b. Supportive commentary on different ways to think or solve a problem ☐

c. Question rules, authority, or societal assumptions while thinking or problem solving ☐

d. Supportive commentary for questioning rules or authority while problem solving ☐

e. Draw different conclusions from the same information ☐

f. Supportive commentary for acknowledging different perspectives ☐

5. Emotions

a. Some age-appropriate emotional complexity is presented ☐

    1. Close to yes ☐

b. Supportive consequences of considering emotional complexity ☐

c. Supportive commentary on emotions expressed ☐

6. PRESENTATIONAL ELEMENTS

a. Opportunities for Active Learning

1. Active Learning Opportunities [A lot(=2), Some(=1), None(=0)] ☐

2. Interactivity [A lot(=2), Some(=1), None(=0)] ☐

3. Scaffolding [This can occur if the material breaks down complex content or draws explicit conclusions] [A lot(=2), Some(=1), None(=0)] ☐

b. Other Positive Presentational Elements

1. Engaging visuals [A lot(=2), Some(=1), None(=0)] ☐

2. Engaging story, plot, or structure [A lot(=2), Some(=1), None(=0)] ☐

3. Engaging language [A lot(=2), Some(=1), None(=0)] ☐

c. Cultural Insensitivity [Significant(=2), Other/possible(=1), None(=0)] ☐

SUMMARY OF WORK WITH ILLUSTRATIONS OF WHY MATERIAL MET
CRITERIA (Use quotes and story description as appropriate)

Key Words for Search:

7. DOES MATERIAL MEET CRITERIA?

*a. **Accept this material** — At least one box is checked in any of these categories: Relationships among Characters, Actions, Thinking, Emotions (NOTE: If characters do not get along throughout box is checked, Supportive Consequences or Supportive Commentary box MUST also be checked in order to check box #2)*

☐

b. Presentational elements (enter total for the six boxes: 0–12)

☐

c. Could not get copyright/permission to use

☐

d. One or more of the four diversity boxes is checked

☐

References

Aboud, F. E. 2003. The formation of in-group favoritism and out-group prejudice in young children: Are they distinct attitudes? *Developmental Psychology 39*(1), January, 48–60.

Aboud, F. E., and Doyle, A. B. 1996. Does talk of race foster prejudice or tolerance in children? *Canadian Journal of Behavioural Science 28*(3), 161–170.

Aboud, F. E., and Fenwick, V. 1999. Exploring and evaluating school-based interventions to reduce prejudice. *Journal of Social Issues 55*(4), Winter, 767–785.

Aboud, F. E., and Levy, S. R. 2000. Interventions to reduce prejudice and discrimination in children and adolescents. In Stuart Oskamp, ed., *Reducing Prejudice and Discrimination*, Mahwah, N.J.: Lawrence Erlbaum Associates, The Claremont Symposium on Applied Social Psychology, 269–293.

Adorno, T. W., Frenkel-Brunswik, E., Levinson, D., and Sanford, R. 1950. *The Authoritarian Personality*, New York: Norton.

Allport, G. W. 1954. *The Nature of Prejudice*. Cambridge, Mass.: Perseus Books.

Arab Republic of Egypt, Ministry of Education. 2007. *National Strategic Plan for Pre-University Education Reform (2007/08–2011/12)*. As of December 26, 2010:
http://planipolis.iiep.unesco.org/upload/Egypt/EgyptStrategicPlanPre-universityEducation.pdf

Bandura, A. 1977. *Social Learning Theory*. Englewood Cliffs, N.J.: Prentice-Hall.

Baumrind, D. 1967. Child care practices anteceding three patterns of preschool behavior. *Genetic Psychology Monographs 75*, 43–88.

———. 1971. Current patterns of parental authority. *Developmental Psychology Monographs 1*, 1–103.

Beck, R. J., and Wood, D. 1993. The dialogic socialization of aggression in a family's court of reason and inquiry. *Discourse Processes 16*(3), July–September, 341–362.

Berry, J. W. 1993. Ethnic identity in plural societies. In M. E. Bernal and G. P. Knight, eds., *Ethnic Formation and Transmission Among Hispanic and Other Minorities,* New York: State University of New York Press, 271–296.

Bigler, R. S., and Liben, L. S. 1993. A cognitive-developmental approach to racial stereotyping and reconstructive memory in Euro-American children. *Child Development, 64*(5), 1507–1518.

Block, C. C. 1993. Strategy instruction in a literature-based reading program. *The Elementary School Journal, Special Issue: Strategies Instruction, 94*(2), November, 139–151.

Bloom, P. 2007. Religion is natural. *Developmental Science, 10*(1), 147–151.

Bouhdiba, A. 1985. *Sexuality in Islam*, London: Routledge and Kegan Paul.

Brewer, D. J., Augustine, C. H., Zellman, G. L., Ryan G. W., Goldman C. A., Stasz, C., and Constant, L. 2007. *Education for a New Era: Design and Implementation of K–12 Education Reform in Qatar*. Santa Monica, Calif.: RAND Corporation, MG-548-QATAR. As of December 26, 2010:
http://www.rand.org/pubs/monographs/MG548.html

Buri, J. 1988. The nature of humankind, authoritarianism and self-esteem. *Journal of Psychology and Christianity, 29*(7), 32–38.

Cantril, H. 1946. The intensity of an attitude. *The Journal of Abnormal and Social Psychology, 41*(2), 129–135.

Carr, K. S. 1988. How can we teach critical thinking? *Childhood Education 65*(2), Winter, 69–71.

Chao, R. 1994. Beyond parental control and authoritarian parenting style. *Child Development 65*, 111–119.

Chomsky, N. 1976. *Reflections on Language*. London: Temple Smith.

Clark, A., Hocevar, D., Dembo, M. H. 1980. The role of cognitive development in children's explanations and preferences for skin color. *Developmental Psychology 16*(4), 332–339.

Clark, K. B., and Clark, M. P. 1947. Racial identification and preference in Negro children. In T.M. Newcomb and E.L. Hartley, eds., *Readings in Social Psychology*. New York: Holt, Rinehart & Winston, 169–178.

Corral-Verdugo, V., Frias-Armenta, M., and Corral-Verdugo, B. A. 1996. Predictors of environmental critical thinking: A study of Mexican children, *Journal of Environmental Education 27*(4), Summer, 23–27.

Cortes, C. E. 1995. Knowledge construction and popular culture: The media as multicultural education. In J. A. Banks and C. A. M. Banks, eds., *Handbook of Research on Multicultural Education*, New York: Macmillan, 211–227.

Crandall, C. S., Eshleman, A., and O'Brien, L. 2002. Social norms and the expression and suppression of prejudice: The struggle for internalization. *Journal of Personality and Social Psychology 82*(3), March, 359–378.

Crisp, R. J., and Turner, R. N. 2009. Can imagined interactions produce positive perceptions? Reducing prejudice through simulated social contact. *American Psychologist, 64*, 231–240.

Crooks, R. C. 1970. The effects of an interracial preschool program upon racial preference, knowledge of racial differences, and racial identification. *Journal of Social Issues, 26*(4), 137–144.

Daniel, M-F., Lafortune, L., Pallascio, R., Mongeau P., Slade, C., Splitter, L., and de la Garza, T. 2003. The development of dialogical critical thinking in children. *Critical Thinking Across the Disciplines 22*(4), Summer pp. 43–55.

Daniel, M-F., Lafortune, L., Pallascio, R., Splitter, L., Slade, C., and de la Garza, T. 2005. Modeling the development process of dialogical critical thinking in pupils aged 10 to 12 years. *Communication Education 54*(4), October, 334–354.

Dawes, A., and Finchilescu, G.. 2002. What's changed? The racial orientations of South African adolescents during rapid political change. *Childhood 9*(2), May, 147–165.

Demircioglu, I. H. 2008. Using historical stories to teach tolerance: The experiences of Turkish eighth-grade students. *Social Studies 99*(3), 105–110.

Downing, J. W., Judd, C. M., and Brauer, M. 1992. Effects of repeated expressions on attitude extremity. *Journal of Personality and Social Psychology, 63*(1), 17–29.

Doyle, A. B., and Aboud, F. E. 1995. A longitudinal study of white children's racial prejudice as a social-cognitive development. *Merrill-Palmer Quarterly: Journal of Developmental Psychology, 41*(2), 209–228.

Edwards, S., and Foss. A. 2000. Using picture books to turn a critical lens on injustice. *New Advocate 13*(4), Fall, 391–393.

el Baz, F. 2007. Reform in Arab countries: The role of education. *Strategic Foresight*, February.

Enright, R. D., and Lapsley, D. K. 1981. Judging others who hold opposite beliefs: The development of belief-discrepancy reasoning. *Child Development, 52*(3), 1053–1063.

Enright, R. D., Lapsley, D. K., Franklin, C. C., and Steuck, K. 1984. Longitudinal and cross-cultural validation of the belief-discrepancy reasoning construct. *Developmental Psychology, 20*(1), 143–149.

Flavell, J. H. 1985. *Cognitive Development* (2nd ed.). Englewood Cliffs. N.J.: Prentice Hall.

Garcia-Coll, C. T., and Vazquez Garcia, H. A. 1995. Developmental processes and their influence on interethnic and interracial relations. In W. D. Hawley and A. W. Jackson, eds., *Toward a Common Destiny: Improving Race and Ethnic Relations in America*. San Francisco: Jossey-Bass, 103–130.

Giancarlo, C. A., Blohm, S. W., and Urdan, T. 2004. Assessing secondary students' disposition toward critical thinking: Development of the California Measure of Mental Motivation. *Educational and Psychological Measurement 64*(2), April, 347–364.

Goodman, M. E. 1952. *Race Awareness in Young Children*. Oxford, UK: Addison-Wesley Press.

Goodman, M. E. 1964. *Race Awareness in Young Children* (revised edition). New York: Collier Press.

Gregg, G. S. 2005. *The Middle East: A Cultural Psychology*, New York: Oxford University Press.

Haidt, J. 2001. The emotional dog and its rational tail: A social intuitionist approach to moral judgment. *Psychological Review 108*(4), October, 814–834.

Halpern, D. F. 1998. Teaching critical thinking for transfer across domains: Dispositions, skills, structure training, and metacognitive monitoring. *American Psychologist, 53*, 449–455.

Hanley, G. F., Heal, N. A., Tiger, J. H., and Ingvarsson, E. T. 2007. Evaluation of a classwide teaching program for developing preschool life skills. *Journal of Applied Behavior Analysis 40*(2), 277–300.

Hastie, B. 2007. Higher education and sociopolitical orientation: The role of social influence in the liberalisation of students, *European Journal of Psychology of Education, Special Issue: Social Psychological Analyses of Educational Dynamics 22*(3), September, 259–274.

The Jordan Education Initiative, 2007. As of December 2, 2010:
http://www.unesco.org/iiep/PDF/pubs/JEI.pdf

Kamii, C. 1991. Toward autonomy: The importance of critical thinking and choice making, *School Psychology Review 20*(3), 382–388.

Katz, J. M. 1983. Altered states of consciousness and emotion. *Imagination, Cognition and Personality, 2*(1), 37–50.

Kohlberg, L. 1976. Moral stages and moralization: The cognitive-development approach. In J. Lickona, ed., *Moral Development Behavior: Theory, Research and Social Issues*. New York: Holt, Rinehart and Winston.

———. 1984. *The Psychology of Moral Development: The Nature and Validity of Moral Judgments* (Vol. 2). New York: Harper & Row.

Marshalidis, S. 2001. Critical thinking in values of education. *Inquiry: Critical Thinking Across the Disciplines 20*, 5–12.

"MBC produces Tash Cartoon and four other series from Dubai Satellite TV," *Asharq al-Awsat* newspaper, October 27, 2006 [In Arabic]. As of January 31, 2011:
http://www.aawsat.com/details.asp?section=25&article=389162&issueno=10195

McAlister, A. L., Ama, E., Barroso, C., Peters, R. J., and Kelder, S. 2000. Promoting tolerance and moral engagement through peer modeling, *Cultural Diversity and Ethnic Minority Psychology 6*(4), November, 363–373.

Moheet.com, 2007. "*The King of Things*, the first Egyptian novel for children, is in its second edition" [In Arabic]. As of January 31, 2011,
http://www.moheet.com/show_news.aspx?nid=67887&pg=12

O'Bryan, M., Fishbein, H. D., and Ritchey, P. N. 2004. Intergenerational transmission of prejudice, sex role stereotyping, and intolerance, *Adolescence 39*(155), Fall, 407–426.

Perkins, D., and Ritchhart, R. 2004. When is good thinking. In D. Y. Dai and R. J. Sternberg, eds., *Motivation, Emotion and Cognition: Integrative Perspectives on Intellectual Functioning and Development*. Mahwah, N.J.: Lawrence Erlbaum Associates, 351–384.

Piaget, J. 1948. *The Moral Judgment of the Child*, Glencoe, Ill.: Free Press.

———. 1983. Piaget's theory. In P. H. Mussen and W. Kessen, eds., *Handbook of Child Psychology*, Vol. 1, *History, Theory and Methods*. New York: Wiley.

Pinker, S. 1994. *The Language of Instinct: How the Mind Creates Language*. New York: William Morrow.

Popp, R. A., Fu, V. R., and Warrell, S. E. 1981. Preschool children's recognition and acceptance of three physical disabilities. *Child Study Journal, 11*, 99–114.

Ramsey, P. G. 1991. The salience of race in young children growing up in an all-white community. *Journal of Educational Psychology, 83*(1), 28–34.

Ramsey, P. G., and Myers, L. C. 1990. Salience of race in young children's cognitive, affective, and behavioral responses to social environments. *Journal of Applied Developmental Psychology, 11*(1), 49–67.

Riesenmy, M. R., Ebel, D., Mitchell, S., and Hudgins, B. B. 1991. Retention and transfer of children's self-directed critical thinking, *Journal of Educational Research 85*(1), September–October, 14–25.

Sadler, W. L. 1993. Awakening student's critical thinking powers through logic problems. *Journal of Instructional Psychology, 20*(4), 359–364.

Sakr, A. 2008. GCC states competing in educational reform. *Arab Reform Bulletin,* May 12.

Schwartz, L. H., Helmus, T. C., Kaye D. D., and Oweidat, N. 2009. *Barriers to the Broad Dissemination of Creative Works in the Arab World,* Santa Monica, Calif.: RAND Corporation, MG-879-OSD. As of December 26, 2010:
http://www.rand.org/pubs/monographs/MG879.html

Scriven, M., and Paul, R. No date. A working definition of *critical thinking.* As of December 26, 2010: http://lonestar.texas.net/~mseifert/crit2.html

Selman, R. 1971. Taking another's perspective: Role-taking development in early childhood. *Child Development, 42*(6), 1721–1734.

Sharabi, H. 1988. *Neopatriarchy.* New York: Oxford University Press.

Simard, D., and Wong, W. 2004. Language awareness and its multiple possibilities for the L2 classroom. *Foreign Language Annals 37*(1), Spring, 96–110.

Skitka, L. J., Bauman, C. W., and Sargis, E. G. 2005. Moral conviction: Another contributor to attitude strength or something more? *Journal of Personality and Social Psychology, 88*(6), 895–917.

Solof, S. B., and Houtz, J. C. 1991. Development of critical thinking among students in kindergarten through Grade 4. *Perceptual and Motor Skills 73*(2), October, 476–478.

Spencer, M. B., and Markstrom-Adams, C. 1990. Identity processes among racial and ethnic minority children in America, *Minority Children, Child Development Special Issue, 61*(2), 290–310.

Sullivan, J., and Transue, J. 1999. The psychological underpinnings of democracy. *Annual Review of Psychology 50,* 625–650.

Thalhammer, K., Wood, S., Bird, K., Avery, P. G., and Sullivan, J. L. 1994. Adolescents and political tolerance: Lip-synching to the tune of democracy. *Review of Education/Pedagogy/Cultural Studies 16,* 325–347.

Trepanier, M. L., and Romatowski, J. A. 1982. Classroom use of selected children's books: Prosocial development in young children. *Journal of Humanistic Counseling, Education, and Development 21*(1), September, 36–42.

UNDP—*See* United Nations Development Programme.

United Nations Development Programme. Various years. Arab Human Development Reports. New York: United Nations Publications. As of February 1, 2011:
http://www.arab-hdr.org/

———. 2003. *Arab Human Development Report 2003: Building a Knowledge Society.* New York: United Nations Publications.

Verkuyten, M., and Slooter, L. 2008. Muslim and non-Muslim adolescents' reasoning about freedom of speech and minority rights. *Child Development, 79*(3), 514–528.

Vogt, W. P. 1997. *Tolerance and Education: Learning to Live with Diversity and Difference.* Thousand Oaks, Calif.: Sage Publications, Inc.

Vygotsky, L. S. 1978. *Mind in Society.* Cambridge. Mass.: Harvard University Press.

Wainryb, C. 1991. Understanding differences in moral judgments: The role of informational assumptions. *Child Development, 62*(4), 840–851.

———. 1993. The application of moral judgments to other cultures: Relativism and universality. *Child Development, 64*(3), 924–933.

Wainryb, C., Shaw, L.A., Laupa, M., and Smith, K. R. 2001. Children's, adolescents', and young adults' thinking about different types of disagreements. *Developmental Psychology 37*(3), 373–386.

Wainryb, C., Shaw, L.A., and Maianu, C. 1998. Tolerance and intolerance: Children's and adolescents' judgments of dissenting beliefs, speech, persons, and conduct. *Child Development 69*(6), December, 541–555.

White, F. A., and Gleitzman, M. 2006. An examination of family socialization processes as moderators of racial prejudice transmission between adolescents and their parents, *Journal of Family Studies 12*(2), November, 247–260.

Willert, J., and Willert, R. 2000. An ignored antidote to school violence: Classrooms that reinforce positive social habits, *American Secondary Education 29*(1), Fall, 27–33.

Wright, J. C., Cullum, J., and Schwab, N. 2008. The cognitive and affective dimensions of moral conviction: Implications for attitudinal and behavioral measures of interpersonal tolerance. *Personality and Social Psychology Bulletin, 34*(11), 1461–1476.

Yee, N., Bailenson, J., and Ducheneaut, N. 2009. The Proteus Effect: Implications of transformed digital self-representation on online and offline behavior. *Communication Research 36*(2), April, 285–312.

Zellman, G. L., Ryan, G., Karam, R., Constant, L., Salem, H., Gonzalez, G., Orr, N., Goldman, C., Al-Thani, H., and Al-Obaidli, K. 2009. *Implementation of the K–12 Education Reform in Qatar's Schools.* Santa Monica: RAND Corporation, MG-880-QATAR. As of December 26, 2010: http://www.rand.org/pubs/monographs/MG880.html

Arabic Materials for Children

'Abd al-Bārī, Ṭāriq, *Malik al-Ashīyā'* ("The King of Things"), Self-published: 2006.

al-Najjār, Taghrīd 'Ārif, *Don't Worry Dad*, Amman, Jordan: Al-Salwa Publishing House, 2007.

———, *The Ogre*, Amman, Jordan: Al-Salwa Publishing House, 2007.

———, *The Story of a Boy Named Fayez*, Beirut, Lebanon: Asala Publishing, 2008.

———, *When the Door Was Knocked*, Amman, Jordan: Al-Salwa Publishing House, 2007.

al-'Awīnī, Hibah, *Lastu Ṣaghīran 'alá al-Ṣiyām* ("I'm Not too Young to Fast"), Malayin, Lebanon: Dar al-'Ilm lilmalayin: 2007.

al-Ba'lbakkī, Fayrūz, *A Street Kid*, Damascus, Syria: Dar al-Fikr, 2007.

Allāh, 'Adlī Rizq, *The Story of Two Trees*, Beirut, Lebanon: Asala Publishing, 2004.

Bashūr, Najlā' Nasīr, *Sha'nūnat al-'Īd* ("Palm Sunday"), Beirut: Mu'sasat Tāla, 2004.

Ben and Izzy, television cartoon, 2008.

Burrāj, Samir Maḥfuẓ, *I Didn't Mean to . . .* , Beirut, Lebanon: Asala Publishing, 2008.

Captain Abu Raed (film in Arabic), 2007.

Dīyyah, Hanādī, *I Live . . . ,* Beirut, Lebanon: Asala Publishing, 2008.

Frīj (Neighborhood), television cartoon produced by Muhammad Sa'īd Hārib, 2007.

Jum'ah, Khālid, *Sheep Don't Eat Cats,* Ramalah: Tamer Institute for Community Education, 2005.

Karākīb, cartoon, written by Aḥmad Sayyid Amīn, 2007.

Khaṭār, Kātī, *I'm the Best Child in the World*, Beirut, Lebanon: Asala Publishing, 2008.

Malātjalīyāt, Mārgū, *The Three Butterflies*, Child World Promotions, 2003.

Mālṭī, Samīr, *And on That Night,* Amman, Jordan: Asala Publishing House, 2009.